POPE FRANCIS

AND THE

NEW VATICAN

POPE FRANCIS
AND THE
NEW VATICAN

PHOTOGRAPHS BY DAVE YODER | ESSAYS BY ROBERT DRAPER

NATIONAL GEOGRAPHIC

WASHINGTON, D.C.

CONTENTS

Previous pages: The open-topped Popemobile carries Pope Francis through a delighted crowd during a Wednesday general audience in St. Peter's Square.

Opposite: Pope Francis, in white cassock and zucchetto, smiles for the faithful at a general audience. "Pray for me," he says, and in turn he is adored.

Following pages: Boys from the Sistine Chapel Choir stand below the high altar of St. Peter's Basilica. *Pages 8–9:* Gray clouds over Vatican City can't dim the hope that Pope Francis, the 266th Bishop of Rome, exudes as he leads the church into the 21st century. *Pages 10–11:* Nuns from the religious order Servants of the Lord and the Virgin of Matará share a laugh while waiting for the pope in the piazza. *Pages 12–13:* Pope Francis embraces a member of his flock during a Wednesday morning general audience. Tens of thousands of people, the faithful and the curious, attend these events.

INTRODUCTION

This book grew out of a growing awareness at National Geographic that we are presently witnessing a seismic revolution in one of the world's great religions. The tremors emanate from the Vatican, which holds sway over the spiritual lives of the planet's 1.2 billion Catholics. It is an ancient institution with a distinct culture that is presently undergoing a profound makeover. The proximate cause of this transformation is of course Pope Francis, a man who cannot be understood without examining his relationship to his birthplace, Argentina. In other words, the story of the Vatican in the time of Pope Francis is much more than a tale of a religious faith and its titular leader. It is, finally, about the interaction between place and culture—the never ending story to which National Geographic is dedicated.

Still, the subject posed unique challenges for a journalist. On the one hand, Pope Francis is a marvel of ubiquity: He makes news seemingly every day, and dozens of books have already been written about him early into his papacy, in addition to countless magazine stories. But the institution he inhabits is opaque in contrast. Before beginning my reporting in the spring of 2014, *National Geographic* Editor in Chief Susan Goldberg, photographer Dave Yoder, and I convened in Rome to discuss the matter with several Vatican officials. At the conclusion of the multicourse lunch, the Vatican officials pledged to support our endeavor. But, cautioned one of them, Archbishop Claudio Maria Celli, there was much more to the ever beaming, refreshingly accessible, and plain-talking new pope than met the eye. An associate who had known

A gate leading to the Vatican Museum frames St. Peter's Basilica.

Day and night, Pope Francis thrives on interacting with the crowd that surrounds him.

Francis for decades, Celli hinted at the man's seemingly contradictory subtleties, as well as ineffable spiritual qualities that eluded easy description. Awarding me a sympathetic smile, the archbishop said, "To capture the feeling of this man Francis . . . well. I will pray for you."

With the help of unusual access and yes, prayer, a magazine story and a book evolved. The material herein draws heavily from interviews I conducted with Vatican officials such as Archbishop Celli during a month-long stay in Rome. I attended numerous public events in which I was able to observe the pope at close proximity. But in researching Francis, I quickly came to learn that those who knew him best were not the inhabitants of Vatican City; rather, they were his fellow *porteños* in Buenos Aires. And so I traveled there as well and was fortunate to spend time with dozens of his longtime friends. From them I learned two basic facts about the man formerly known as Jorge Bergoglio, or Padre Jorge. First, the new Pope is in fact instantly recognizable to Argentines. And second, he is full of surprises—of which we are likely to see more.

The lushness and humanity you see reflected in these pages are testament to the talent, heart, and sheer professionalism of David Yoder. A resident of Rome, Dave spent literally months inside the walls of the Vatican, patiently shadowing Pope Francis while also memorializing the timeless beauty within Vatican City.

Together with his moving visuals and my reporting, we have sought to capture a remarkable moment in the history of human spirituality—one in which a single individual has used the simplest of messages to alter a dominant world religion in a host of complicated ways.

THE NEW
VATICAN

"**I** really need to start making changes right now." • Pope Francis spoke these words in late May 2013, a mere two months after the Vatican conclave had vaulted the former Cardinal Jorge Mario Bergoglio of Argentina from obscurity into the papacy. His guests that morning at his humble papal residence of Santa Marta, inside the walls of Vatican City, were a half dozen of his friends who were visiting from back home in Buenos Aires. • To them, his confidential sentiments were both remarkable and thoroughly unsurprising: remarkable, because to many observers—some delighted, others discomfited—Pope Francis had already changed seemingly everything, seemingly overnight. He was the first Latin American pope. The first Jesuit pope. The first non-European-born pope in more than a thousand years. The first pope to take the moniker of St. Francis of Assisi, champion of the poor.

A VOTE FOR CHANGE

No one saw him coming; perhaps even those cardinals who voted for him did not know what they were getting. Like his colleagues, Bergoglio had arrived in Rome a couple of weeks prior to the March 12 conclave. Nothing about the bespectacled, 76-year-old Argentine conveyed the slightest aura of distinction. He was just another elderly passenger seated in economy class on an Alitalia plane who happened to be wearing the simple black attire of a parish priest, without any of the red regalia that would mark him as the cardinal he happened to be.

Upon his arrival, the Archbishop of Buenos Aires checked into a hotel designated for clergy on via della Scrofa, in the heart of heavily touristed Old Rome. He traveled each day to the pre-conclave meetings at the Vatican by taxi—(or, weather permitting, on foot)—eschewing, as he always had, the regal insulation of chauffeur-driven sedans that most bishops preferred. He wanted to be closer to the way normal people lived their lives.

The subtext of these meetings was the fallout over Pope Benedict XVI's abrupt resignation on February 11, 2013. The then pope had frankly declared in a statement that at the age of 85, he no longer possessed the wherewithal to manage the Church's myriad challenges. Those challenges included an unattractive litany of financial and sexual scandals. To many cardinals, such episodes bespoke the need for a new approach altogether: not simply a new pope but also a new leader who would cast aside the Church's aloofness and expand its spiritual constituency. Cardinal Peter Turkson of Ghana recalls: "Just before the conclave, when all the cardinals gathered, we shared our views. There was a certain mood: Let's get a change. That kind of mood was strong inside. No one said, 'No more Italians or no more Europeans'—but a desire for change was there.

"Cardinal Bergoglio was basically unknown to all those gathered there. But then he gave a talk—it was kind of his own manifesto. He advised those of us gathered that we need to think about the Church that goes out to the periphery—not just geographically, but to the periphery of human existence. For him, the Gospel invites us all to have that sort of sensitivity. That was his contribution. And it brought a sort of freshness to the exercise of pastoral care, a different experience of taking care of God's people."

Among the reporters who cover the Vatican—the so-called *Vaticanisti,* a seasoned and usually shrewd press corps that treats its beat as almost totally secular —Bergoglio was not regarded as *papabile,* or pope-worthy. Though he had been the surprise runner-up to Joseph Ratzinger (Pope Benedict XVI) in the 2005 conclave following the death of Pope John Paul II, Bergoglio was now considered too old, his previous star turn deemed an electoral fluke unlikely to be repeated in 2013. There were other, buzzier contenders—among them the shrewd Italian cardinal, Angelo Scola, and another Latin American, Cardinal Odilo Scherer of Brazil.

Only Catholic News Service bureau chief John Thavis had the prescience to sense otherwise. As Thavis wrote one day before the conclave began: "In the last few days, some serious voices have mentioned Cardinal Bergoglio as a contender in the coming conclave. Not simply because he came in second the last time around, but because he impressed Cardinals when he took the floor in the pre-Conclave meetings that began last week. His words left the impression that even at age 76, Bergoglio had the energy and the inclination to do some house-cleaning in the Roman Curia [the central governing body through which the Pope oversees the Catholic Church]. This conclave has multiple contenders but no real front-runner, and it's quite possible that if early voting produces a stall, the College of Cardinals could once again turn to Cardinal Bergoglio as someone who would bring key changes but without an extra-long reign."

The surprise outcome instantly begat a succession of surprises. Moments after his election on the evening

Pope Francis greets Pope Emeritus Benedict (left) at an October 2014 Mass celebrating the end of the Synod on the Family, an assembly of bishops that assists the pope in addressing questions facing the Church.

of March 13, 2013, the new leader of the Catholic Church materialized from the balcony of St. Peter's Basilica in Vatican City without the traditional red scarf known as the mozzetta, wearing a silver pectoral cross around his neck instead of the usual gold embroidery. He greeted the screaming masses below with electrifying plainness: "*Buona sera, fratelli e sorelle* (Good evening, brothers and sisters)." He introduced himself not as the pope, but as the Bishop of Rome. And he closed with a request, what many Argentines already knew to be his signature line: "Pray for me." When he departed the ceremonies, he walked past the limousine that awaited him and hopped into the bus ferrying the cardinals who had just made him their superior.

The next morning, the new pope paid his bill at the Rome hotel where he had been staying. Forswearing the vastness of the traditional papal apartment inside the Apostolic Palace, he elected as his permanent living quarters an austere two-bedroom dwelling in Suite 201 of Domus Sanctae Marthae, or Santa Marta—named for Martha of Bethany, sister of Mary and Lazarus. In his first meeting with the international press, he declared his primary ambition: "Oh, how I would like a poor Church, and for the poor." And instead of celebrating the first Holy Thursday Mass of his papacy (commemorating the Last Supper) at St. Peter's Basilica, he spent it washing and kissing the feet of 12 inmates at a youth prison on the outskirts of Rome.

All of this took place during his first month as the Holy Eminence of Vatican City.

And yet that morning in late May, the new pope's Argentine friends understood what he really meant by "changes." While even the smallest of his gestures carried considerable weight, the man they knew was not content to be a purveyor of symbols. He was a practical *callejero,* a street priest who wanted the Catholic Church to make a lasting difference in people's lives—to be, as he often put it, a hospital on a battlefield, taking in all who were wounded, regardless of their affiliation. In the pursuit of this objective, he could be, according to Argentine rabbi and friend Abraham Skorka, "a very stubborn person."

BECOMING FRANCIS

Though to the outside world Pope Francis seemed to have exploded out of the skies like a meteor shower, he was a well-known and occasionally controversial religious figure back home. The son of a working-class accountant whose family had emigrated from northwestern Italy's Piedmont region, Bergoglio had distinguished himself from the moment he entered the seminary in 1957 at the age of 20 (after briefly but famously working as a lab technician and as a bouncer at a club). In 1958 he chose the intellectually challenging and socially rigorous Society of Jesus as his path to the priesthood. He taught unruly boys, washed the feet of prisoners, and studied overseas. He became the rector of Colegio Maximo as well as a fixture in the blighted shantytowns throughout Buenos Aires. And he rose in the Jesuit hierarchy even while navigating the murky politics of an era that saw the Catholic Church enter into fraught relationships: first with Juan Perón—the thrice-elected president of Argentina who sought to dignify labor—and later the military dictatorship that ousted Perón.

He fell out of favor with his Jesuit superiors, then just as quickly, an admiring cardinal plucked him from exile and helped make him bishop in 1992. He rose to become archbishop in 1998 and cardinal in 2001. Shy in disposition, Bergoglio preferred the company of the poor over the affluent. His indulgences were few: literature, soccer, tango music, and gnocchi. Still, for all his simplicity, the Argentine was an urban animal, an acute social observer, and, in his quiet way, a natural leader. Though typically averse to publicity, Bergoglio would seize a moment when he sensed the need to do so.

His papacy was not mere coincidence. As the Roman author Massimo Franco would put it, "This pope is the son of the resignation"—referring to the sudden (and, for the past six hundred years, unprecedented) resignation from the papacy by Benedict, a bookish theologian with long experience in the Vatican but little as a crisis manager. His departure brought into relief the mounting sentiment that the Church was beset by peril—that the hoary and insular Eurocentric mind-set of the Holy See (the office of the Catholic Church in Rome) was rotting from within. Bergoglio's assumption of the papacy reflected this crisis mentality, says Franco: "His election arose from a trauma."

Sitting in the living room of his apartment at Santa Marta that morning in May, the pope acknowledged to his old friends the daunting challenges that awaited him: *Financial disarray in the Vatican's Institute for the Works of Religion (colloquially referred to as the Vatican Bank). Bureaucratic greed bedeviling the Roman Curia. Continuing disclosures of pedophilic priests who are insulated from justice by Vatican officials.* Juxtaposed against the moral strictness of a highly ritualized religious order, the Church's hypocrisies risked alienating an entire generation of Christians.

On these and other matters, Francis intended to move boldly. Though he had not asked to be pope, the moment the name Jorge Bergoglio had been called out in the conclave, he felt a tremendous sense of peace. And, he told his friends, "To this day, I still feel the same peace."

THE POPE'S PARADOX

Pope Francis is, according to the international press, a reformer. A radical. A revolutionary. And also none of these things.

His impact on the world thus far is as impossible to miss as it is impossible to measure. More than any figure in recent memory, Francis has kindled a spiritual spark among not only Catholics but also other Christians, those of other faiths, and even nonbelievers.

As Rabbi Abraham Skorka says, "He is changing religiosity throughout the world."

More acutely, the new leader of the Catholic Church is widely seen as good news for an institution that, prior to his arrival, had known only bad news days. "Two years ago," says Father Thomas J. Reese, a senior analyst at the *National Catholic Reporter,* "if you asked anybody on the street, 'What's the Catholic Church for and against,' you would've gotten: 'It's against gay marriage, against birth control'—all this stuff. Now if you ask people, they'll say, 'Oh, the pope—he's the guy who loves the poor and doesn't live in a palace.' That's an extraordinary achievement for such an old institution. I jokingly say that Harvard Business School could use him to teach rebranding. And politicians in Washington would kill for his approval rating."

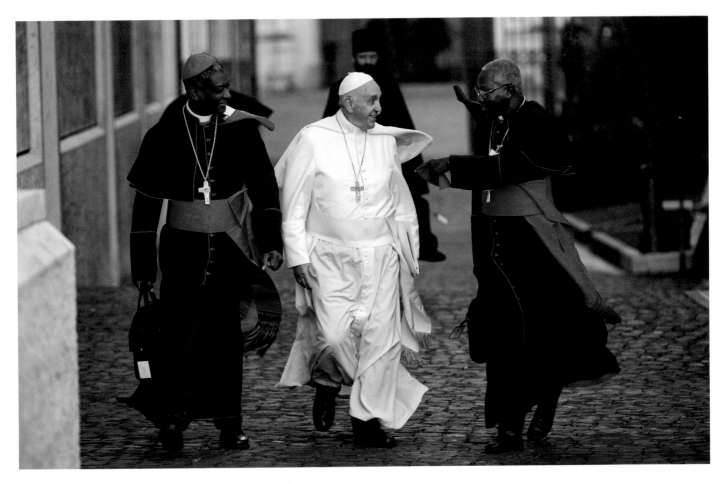

Two cardinals share time with the pontiff during the Synod on the Family.

The sight of him is unforgettable: Warm-eyed with an effortless smile, he cuts a figure of encompassing radiance that not even the most adroit retail politician could replicate. This incandescent spectacle is something of a surprise to his old friends, who remember him, says one, as "so reserved, not terribly happy." To Martin Murphy, a former student, the explanation is simple: "He's having fun with this. He enjoys it." But a third Argentine friend, Father Pepe di Paola, suggested during a visit with Francis in August 2013 that something deeper was at work. "You're the same person with the same convictions, but something has changed in you—your gestures and your ability to communicate are completely different, and I believe this is the work of the Holy Spirit," the priest told the pope, who nodded in reply. More notably, we see this in Pope Francis because he is in fact there to be seen. He has aggressively sought to be what Massimo Franco calls the "available pope—a contradiction in terms."

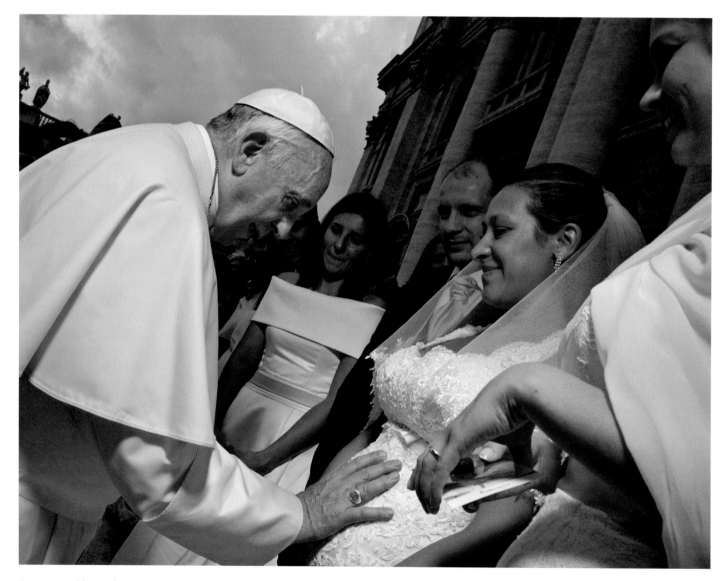

Pope Francis blesses the unborn child of a bride. Newlyweds attending a weekly Wednesday audience can sit in a special section to receive the papal blessing.

His corporeal accessibility conveys something more meaningful than a photo op.

His availability has been received with the kind of delirium one ordinarily associates with teen idols. Of course, as is evident when speaking to Vatican officials, the spectacle of a papal personality cult—Francis as rock star—is beneath the dignity of the Church. (There is no evidence that the pope himself relishes such celebrity. At the same time, notes veteran Reuters *Vaticanista* Philip Pullella, "The crowd has a very medicinal effect on him. He'll look really tired, and then they just light him up.") His sheer exposure to the masses is both wondrous and, to those who admire him—not to mention his security team—more than a little unnerving. As one of his old friends, Argentine Pentecostal pastor and scholar Dr. Norberto Saracco, said to him during a visit to Santa Marta, "Jorge, we know that you don't wear a bulletproof vest. There are many crazy people out there."

Francis replied calmly, "The Lord has put me here. He'll have to look out for me."

His corporeal accessibility conveys something more meaningful than a photo op. It is the conscious recognition of a *callejero* who, like his namesake Francis of Assisi, has long believed that the Church must go out into the world, and not vice versa. Those who understand the Jesuit order—with its emphasis on communal engagement, preceded by a program of rigorous reflection known as the Spiritual Exercises— see this as the most telling trait of Francis's papacy thus far. "The radical difference comes from his own experiences with the exercises of St. Ignatius [the founder of the Jesuit order]," says Jose Luis Lorenzatti, a former student of the pope's. "From my experience in the order, these exercises enable you to follow the direction set by the Holy Spirit in a deeper way. This is the necessary difference between Francis and Pope Benedict. The Jesuit influence is absolutely distinct."

"Think of the parable of the Good Samaritan, of confronting a wounded person in the road," says Archbishop Claudio Maria Celli. "The message of this is not just to approach and analyze. It is reaching out—the pope's famous 'culture of the encounter.' " And, Celli points out, the pope has deliberately set an example for the Church by gravitating toward the pronouncedly wounded. The images of His Holiness bending down to kiss the wheelchair-bound and physically disfigured at Wednesday Mass in St. Peter's Square have cut through the quotidian visual clutter like arrows of an indelible truth.

"What is clear is that he eliminates every sense of distance," says Father Federico Lombardi, the head of the Vatican's press office. "When he speaks to you, he is meeting you—he is interested in you as a person, not, say, as a journalist." Though throughout his life Jorge Bergoglio had shown a reluctance to give interviews to the media, whenever he did so, says Buenos Aires–based journalist Francesca Ambrogetti (who spoke to the then archbishop numerous times for a book she co-wrote with Sergio Rubin), "He answered everything—and not by turning the question around into something he'd prefer to answer."

The decidedly unstarry-eyed *Vaticanisti* were stunned to see this for themselves at the conclusion of the pope's first overseas trip in July 2013, to Brazil. On the flight back home, Francis instructed Lombardi to tell the traveling press that he would be happy to take any questions, regardless of subject. When an

Italian journalist brought up the much discussed spectacle of the pope carrying his own black briefcase onto the plane—something that, the reporter said, had never been done before, Francis replied with a grin, "It wasn't the key for the atom bomb!" He then added, bashfully but earnestly, "I don't know . . . What you say is a bit strange for me, that the photograph went all over the world. But we must get used to being normal. The normality of life."

This "culture of the encounter" that large audiences and small press pools have witnessed in Pope Francis is seen as well by eminences throughout the world—to an unorthodox effect. Says communications director Lombardi, "I always meet with the pope after every audience he has had with heads of state. I ask him if there's anything from their meeting that he would like for me to communicate. And what I see is what

he's looking for in these meetings with politicians is an encounter with the complete person."

Referring to similar debriefings he used to have with Francis's predecessor, Lombardi continues, "Benedict was so clear. He would say, 'We have spoken about these things, I agree with these points, I would argue against these other points, the objective of our next meeting will be this'—two minutes and I'm totally clear about what the contents were. With Francis— 'This is a wise man, he has had these interesting experiences.' Diplomacy for Francis is not so much strategy, but instead, 'I have met this person, we now have a personal relation, let us now do good for the people and for the Church.' "

More than any public figure in recent memory, Pope Francis evinces a mesmerizing gift for plain yet penetrating speech. Seemingly every utterance reveals the

Pope Francis talks with the prefect of the papal household, Archbishop Georg Gänswein. The pontiff's blue Ford Focus is visible behind him.

It is the very fact of Francis: his papal aura reimagined as an approachable simplicity.

two-sided coin of his persona: working-class *porteño* (the common term for a Buenos Aires lifer) and intellectually rigorous Jesuit. Because his words carry such lingering resonance, they have become a kind of Rorschach test: The ideologically inclined hear in his aphorisms what they wish. His instantly iconic and seemingly off-the-cuff rejoinder to a question about gay priests—"Who am I to judge?"—elated some progressive Catholics who surmised that he might eventually endorse same-sex marriage. Similarly, old-school Catholics were heartened to hear him remark, in the wake of an Islamic extremist group's massacre of employees at *Charlie Hebdo* (a French publication that regularly satirized the Prophet Muhammad), that freedom of expression had its limits: "If my good friend . . . says a curse word against my mother, he can expect a punch. It's normal."

Yet the likelihood that Pope Francis will radically alter Catholic doctrine approximates the chances that he will ever advocate violent revenge. What seems instead to rivet audiences throughout the world, from St. Peter's Square to the streets of Colombo, Sri Lanka, is a message more basic than speech itself. It is the very fact of Francis: the blinding whiteness of his papal aura reimagined as an approachable simplicity. It is the fact of His Holiness countering the adoration of the masses with the humblest of dares: "Pray for me." It is his refusal to be adored, and to adore instead—to kiss the hand of a martyr, to weep openly in the martyr's arms, implicitly saying: *I will never be as holy as you*. It is the fact of the pope as a model of vulnerability.

It is *el encuentro,* the encounter—a decidedly more arduous feat of outreach and inclusion than the impersonal laying down of edicts. For it is the laying down of all pretense, complete self-exposure.

Available pope—a contradiction in terms.

AN EVOLVING LEGACY

When Federico Wals, who had spent several years as Cardinal Bergoglio's press aide, traveled from Buenos Aires to Rome last year to see the pope, he first paid a visit to Father Federico Lombardi, whose job at the Vatican essentially mirrors Wals's old one, albeit on a much larger scale. "So, Father," the Argentine asked, "how do you feel about my former boss?"

Managing a smile, Lombardi replied, "Confused."

For those who wanted change, Pope Francis has not disappointed. He has appointed 39 new cardinals, 24 of whom come from outside Europe. With a searing speech in December 2014 in which he ticked off the "sicknesses" afflicting the Curia (among them, "vainglory," "gossip," and "worldly profit"), the Pope has tasked nine cardinals—all but two of them outsiders to the curia—with reforming the administrative institution. Calling sexual abuse in the Church a "sacrilegious cult," he has formed a Pontifical Commission for the Protection of Minors headed by Seán Patrick O'Malley, Archbishop of Boston. He moved swiftly to defrock an Iowa priest accused of committing indecent acts decades ago, as well as to fire a Paraguayan bishop for covering up the acts of a molesting priest.

In an effort to bring transparency to the Vatican Bank, the pope brought in a tough former rugby player, Cardinal George Pell of Sydney, Australia, and named him Secretariat of the Economy—a designation that

puts Pell on a par with the Secretary of State, Cardinal Pietro Parolin. Amid these appointments, the pope has paid a single act of deference to the old guard: He has kept in place—at least for now—Cardinal Gerhard Müller, Pope Benedict's hard-line appointee to head the Vatican's "holy office," the Congregation for the Doctrine of the Faith (which, as its name implies, clarifies and enforces Church doctrine).

Such moves signify much—but it is hard to say what, if anything, they will lead to. The early clues have been tantalizing both to reformists and to more traditional Catholics. The preliminary Synod on the Family that Francis convened in October 2014 produced no sweeping doctrinal changes, which mollified conservative Catholics who feared exactly that. But the actual synod in October 2015 could produce a dramatically different outcome.

According to one of the pope's friends and former instructors, Juan Carlos Scannone of the Jesuit seminary of San Miguel, "On the subject of divorced and remarried couples [taking Communion], he told me, 'I want to listen to everyone.' He's going to wait for the second synod, and he'll listen to everyone, but he's definitely open to a change." Another friend discussed with the pope the possibility of removing celibacy as a requirement for priests. That friend says, "If he can survive the pressures of the Church today and the results of the Synod on the Family next October, I think after that he will be ready to talk about celibacy."

Such guesses, though educated, are only that. As Vatican officials take measure of their new leader, it is tempting for them to view the pope's open-hearted public mannerisms as evidence that he is a creature of pure spiritual instinct. "Totally spontaneous," Father Lombardi said, for example, of Francis's series of much analyzed gestures during his spring 2014 trip to the Middle East—among them, his embrace of an imam and a rabbi after praying together with them at the Western Wall.

His friend Abraham Skorka admits that this act was in fact premeditated—Francis having known before he embarked for the Holy Land that it was the rabbi's dream to embrace the pope and Omar Abboud, the imam, beside the wall. That Francis agreed in advance to fulfill the rabbi's wish makes the gesture no less heartfelt. Instead, it suggests an awareness on his part that his every twitch and syllable will be parsed for symbolic portent. Such prudence is thoroughly in keeping with the Jorge Bergoglio who in 2007 told the journalists Francesca Ambrogetti and Sergio Rubin that he seldom heeded his impulses, since "the first answer that comes to me is usually wrong." (He also told them that if his house were on fire, he would take two items with him: his breviary, or book of Catholic liturgical rites, and his appointment book.)

Those who have known him the longest scoff at any suggestion that Pope Francis is flying by the seat of his pants. During his days at the Archdiocese of Buenos Aires, Wals recalls, "Everything was perfectly organized. I knew when he'd be in his office, how long his appointments would take, and how long his speeches would be." Rogelio Pfirter, a leading Argentine diplomat who has remained close to Bergoglio since being his boarding school student a half century ago, agrees. "When you read about him improvising, and this very chaotic agenda—I don't think that's the case at all. I think he knows very well what he's doing. Each and every step has been thought out."

"He's a chess player," says Ramiro de la Serna, a Buenos Aires–area Franciscan priest who was one of the pope's college students more than 30 years ago and has remained close to him since. "That is not to say that he's insincere. He's true to himself. But he understands the consequences of what he says and does. He's cognizant of reality. For example, after he was elected pope and told the international media he wanted 'a poor Church for the poor'—he knew that

Pope Francis greets a bishop as he walks into the assembly hall during the Synod on the Family.

within two minutes, this phrase would lead the headlines all over the world."

Correspondingly, Pope Francis is aware that any slip of the tongue or misstep on his part will also make headlines. As archbishop in 2010, he was personally stung when a letter he had written in confidence to several Argentine nuns, asking for their support in opposing legislation that would permit same-sex marriage, was leaked to and (in his view) grossly distorted by the press. And, like any cardinal, he was familiar with the disclosure in 2012 of several Vatican internal documents alleging corruption and thereby giving rise to the so-called Vatileaks scandal. If Pope Francis harbored concrete plans for changing long-held Catholic beliefs and traditions, it would therefore stand to reason that he would not spell them out, even to his closest associates.

Then again, who knows? In October 2013, the pope happened to read a provocative column written by Eugenio Scalfari, the atheist founder of *La Repubblica*. Francis then called Scalfari and offered himself up for an in-person interview—one in which he criticized the Roman Curia for having a "Vatican-centric view" that "neglects the world around us," adding, "I do not share this view, and I'll do everything I can to change it." Similarly, after receiving a letter from an Argentine woman who wished to marry a divorced man, the pope called her out of the blue in April 2014. According to the woman, Francis assured her that "there was no problem" in divorced couples taking Communion. Were these unrecorded conversations accurate? Were his remarks extemporaneous, or carefully thought through?

Inside the Vatican, the preoccupation of reading the papal tea leaves has been made more difficult by the pope's determination to be his own man—which means, among other things, being his own scheduler. "No one knows all of what he's doing," Lombardi says of Francis. "His personal secretary doesn't even know. I have to call around: One person knows one part of his schedule, someone else knows another part. Before, it was different. I could call [Pope John Paul II's personal secretary Stanisław] Dziwisz, or [Pope Benedict's top assistant Georg] Gänswein, and they would always know. Sometimes the pope will say, 'Father, I have met with this person.' But not in a systematic way. This is the life."

In attempting to divine Francis's intentions, the closest thing Vatican officials have to an intermediary has been Secretary of State Cardinal Pietro Parolin. Parolin is a much respected pastor, a veteran diplomat, and among his boss's most trusted confidants, according to Federico Wals, "because he's not too ambitious.

That's a fundamental quality for the pope." At the same time, the pope has drastically reduced the secretary of state's powers, particularly with respect to the Vatican's finances, to prevent excesses like those Parolin's predecessor—the Machiavellian Tarcisio Bertone—displayed during Benedict's papacy. (Bertone was accused of cronyism and of misappropriating millions of dollars in the Vatican Bank.)

"The problem with this," Lombardi says, "is that the structure of the Curia is no longer clear. The process is ongoing, and what will be at the end, no one knows. The secretary of state is not as centralized, and the pope has many relations that are directed by him alone, without any mediation." Valiantly accentuating the upside, the Vatican spokesman adds, "In a sense, this is positive, because in the past there were criticisms that someone had too much power over the pope. They cannot say this is the case now."

Life in the Holy See was altogether different under Benedict, a cerebral scholar who continued to write theological books during his eight years as pope. It was different, too, under his mentor John Paul II, a theatrically trained performer and accomplished linguist whose papacy lasted 27 years (following John Paul I, who died in 1978 after only 33 days on the job). Both men were reliable keepers of papal orthodoxy, extending to their kingly trappings—John Paul II with his Rolex, Benedict with his custom-made cologne. The spectacle of this new pope, with his cheap plastic watch and bulky black orthopedic shoes, taking his breakfast in the Vatican cafeteria alongside nuns and janitors, has required some adjustment for those who have long taken comfort in centuries of papal predictability.

In certain ways, Francis is a throwback. He begins his mornings at about 4 a.m., with prayer. He has never owned a cell phone. (News of Pope Benedict's resignation reached him a day late because of this.) For that matter, he has never used the Internet;

A glass trinket is one of many keepsakes on sale near Vatican City.

instead, he replies to emails in his microscopic handwriting, which his private secretary then reproduces on a computer. (The tweets on his @Pontifex Twitter account, which has more than five million followers, are written by the Vatican press office.) Still, his *porteño* irreverence is a striking contrast to the quasi-imperial trappings around him.

His informality is best exemplified by his sense of humor—which, though sly and often ironic, is never mean. After being visited in Santa Marta by his old friend Archbishop Claudio Maria Celli, Francis insisted on accompanying his guest to the elevator.

"Why is this?" Celli asked with a smile. "So that you can be sure that I'm gone?"

Without missing a beat, the pope added, "And so that I can be sure you don't take anything with you."

PURE GRACE

Yet even in levity, Francis is ever conscious of the difficulties he confronts as he seeks to inculcate the culture of the encounter into the Catholic Church. As he told his close friend Jorge Milia, an Argentine journalist, last year: "There's no user's manual. So I do as I can."

For all of the seemingly drastic changes Francis has brought to his papacy, he has made some common-sense concessions to the institutional realities of the Vatican as well. Though he has told the Swiss Guard that they do not need to stand outside his door at night or accompany him to the elevator, he is otherwise resigned to their near-constant presence. (He often uses the guards to take his photograph with visiting friends—another concession to his present status, since Jorge Bergoglio has long recoiled from cameras.) The pope recognizes that he can no longer ride the subways and mingle in the ghettos as he was famed for doing in Buenos Aires. He lamented during a press conference four months after he assumed the papacy,

"You know how often I've wanted to go walking through the streets of Rome—because in Buenos Aires, I liked to go for a walk in the city; I really liked to do that. In this sense, I feel a little penned in."

Though it has never been his way to mingle with politicians, as the head of the Vatican and as an Argentine he has felt duty-bound to receive his country's president, Cristina Fernández de Kirchner, even when it has been painfully evident that she has used these visits for her own political gain. (And when, to his annoyance, Kirchner showed up in September 2014 to Santa Marta with more than 40 of her friends.) "When Bergoglio received the president in a friendly way, it was out of pure grace," says one of his friends, Buenos Aires Evangelical minister Juan Pablo Bongarra. "She didn't deserve it. But that's how God loves us, with pure grace." Perhaps one could say that this is ultimately the mission of Pope Francis—to ignite a revolution of grace, inside the Vatican and well beyond its walls, without altering a single precept. "He won't change doctrine," insists his Argentine friend, the Franciscan priest Ramiro de la Serna. "What he will do is return the Church to its true doctrine—the one it has forgotten, the one that puts man back in the center. For too long, the Church put sin in the center. By putting the suffering of man, and his relationship with God, back in the center, these harsh attitudes towards homosexuality, divorce, and other things will start to change."

This revolution—whether or not it succeeds—is unlike any other, if only for the relentless joy with which it has been waged. When the new Archbishop of Buenos Aires, Cardinal Mario Poli, commented to Francis during a visit to Vatican City about how remarkable it was to see his once dour old friend now wearing an omnipresent smile, the resident at Santa Marta considered those words carefully, as he always does.

Then Francis said with, one imagines, a smile: "It's very entertaining, being the pope."

A
PLACE
like no
OTHER

✠

Embodying millennia of history,
the Vatican is a physical and spiritual
cornerstone of Christendom.
Each year, millions journey to the
breathtakingly adorned St. Peter's
Basilica and adjoining piazza to
observe the ceremonial traditions and
artistic masterpieces that make it
sacred. From the Sala Regia to the
Swiss Guard's barracks, the city is
an endless source of wonder.

Let the Church always be a place
of mercy and hope, where everyone
is welcomed, loved and forgiven.

POPE FRANCIS

Faith is not a light which scatters all our darkness, but a lamp which guides our steps in the night and suffices for the journey.

POPE FRANCIS

Father Bruno Silvestrini, the pastor of the Vatican's Church of St. Anne, leads a Mass at a machine shop on Vatican City grounds.

Previous pages: St. Peter's curving colonnades form two semicircles, which the 17th-century architect Gian Lorenzo Bernini said gave the portico an "open-armed, maternal welcome" to pilgrims.

Music fills the air during an inaugural Mass for the start of the Vatican's judicial year, held in the Church of St. Mary, a small chapel within Vatican City walls.

We need to practice the art of listening, which is more than simply hearing. Listening, in communication, is an openness of heart which makes possible that closeness without which genuine spiritual encounter cannot occur. Listening helps us to find the right gesture and word which shows that we are more than simply bystanders.

POPE FRANCIS

Holiness doesn't mean doing extraordinary things, but doing ordinary things with love and faith.

POPE FRANCIS

Above: It takes a village to keep the Vatican running. A nun who works in the Apostolic Sacristy helps a priest don his robes.

Pope Francis warmly greets clergy in the Chapel of the Pietà (named for Michelangelo's marble sculpture) before an outdoor Mass.

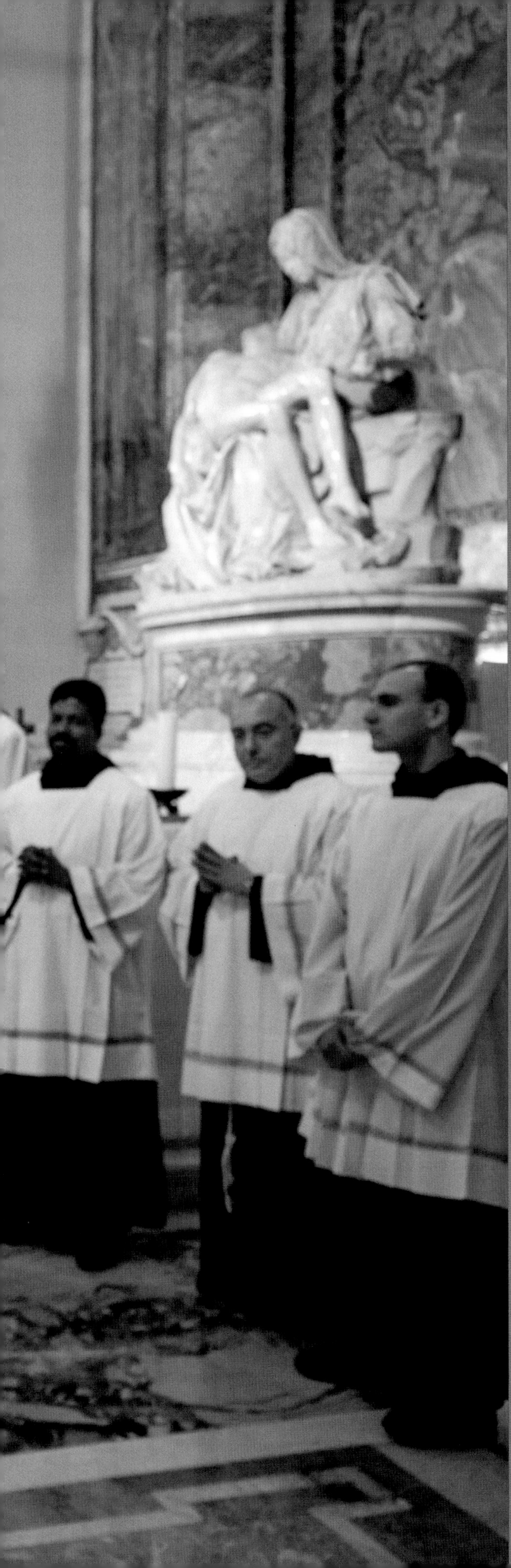

There was a warmth and gentleness that immediately drew people to him and made people smile back with warmth and affection.

ARCHBISHOP FRANCIS A. CHULLIKATT

A pair of Sardinian mules look less than
pleased at being given to the pontiff.
Little do they know that they're destined
to join others at the 136-acre papal estate,
the Villas of Castel Gandolfo.

Having faith does
not mean having no
difficulties, but having
the strength to
face them, knowing
we are not alone.

POPE FRANCIS

Below: At the inside edge of St. Peter's Square, Swiss Guards watch over an entrance beside the basilica.

Opposite: Members of the Pontifical Swiss Guard put on their armor. All guards come from the regular Swiss army.

Rare is the leader who makes us want to be better people. Pope Francis is such a leader.

PRESIDENT BARACK OBAMA

My mission of being
in the heart of the people
is not just a part of my life
or a badge I can take off;
it is not an "extra" or just
another moment in life.
Instead, it is something
I cannot uproot from my
being without destroying
my very self. I am a
mission on this earth; that
is the reason why I am
here in this world.

POPE FRANCIS

Previous pages: Swiss Guards escort the president of Egypt, Abdel Fattah al-Sisi, through the Sala Clementina in the Apostolic Palace.

The pontiff uses his open-topped Popemobile to mingle with the crowds that gather in St. Peter's Square.

The ministers of the Gospel must
be people who can warm the
hearts of the people, who walk
through the dark night with them,
who know how to dialogue
and to descend themselves into
their people's night, into the
darkness, but without getting lost.
The people of God want pastors,
not clergy acting like bureaucrats
or government officials.

POPE FRANCIS

Above: Vatican staff prepare the balcony from which the pope will address the crowd in St. Peter's Square.

Below: St. Peter's Square comes alive for the Christmas season, with a nativity scene and sparkling Christmas tree.

Following pages: A lone Swiss Guard patrols Bernini's Scala Regia, the monumental staircase connecting the Apostolic Palace with the basilica. Now that the pope no longer lives in the palace, the corridors carry much less pedestrian traffic.

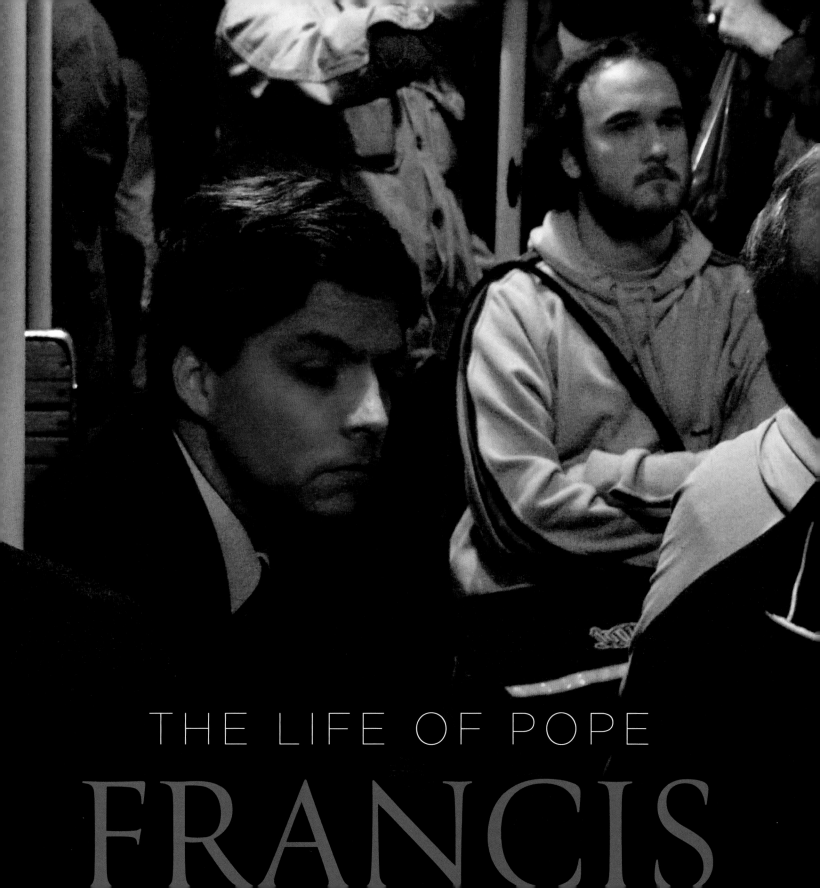

THE LIFE OF POPE

FRANCIS

Previous pages: Known for being streetwise, then Cardinal Jorge Mario Bergoglio (second from left) rides the subway in Buenos Aires, Argentina, in 2008.

Pope Francis seems most comfortable when mingling with his flock.

On the morning of March 14, 2013, a middle-age man was sitting on a bench in a shopping mall just outside Washington D.C., crying his eyes out, when he wife came up and asked him, "What's wrong? What just happened?" • Still sobbing, the man held out his iPad: "Look at the news!" he managed in joy and disbelief. "Jorge is pope!" • Nearly a half century earlier, in 1964, the man had been a student of Jorge Mario Bergoglio, at the Institute of the Immaculate Conception in Santa Fe, Argentina. For him and his peers, the man they called Padre Jorge was far more than a literature and philosophy teacher. He talked to them about their writing, their families, their ambitions, soccer, girls. At 27 years old, not yet a priest and in his first year as a teacher, Bergoglio seemed reflexively all-knowing. (They had no idea how feverishly he had prepared for his class lectures.) Most of all, he seemed all-caring.

Still, the pope who today emphasizes the Church's "maternal attitude" was especially influenced by the women of his youth.

The man weeping in the mall knew this better than others. Padre Jorge had been his spiritual adviser. One day the boy screwed up the courage to share a deep concern. He suffered a medical condition in his groin that, he worried, would make it impossible for him to have children someday. He feared that playing soccer would aggravate the condition. The 15-year-old boy wondered if his prospects for a normal life were doomed.

Padre Jorge listened carefully, as he always did. He offered supportive words. And then he began to gather books about the boy's condition. He met with a scientific expert. The evidence he had amassed convinced the boy he had nothing to worry about. About 15 years later, Bergoglio officiated the young man's wedding. Not long after that, he gave Communion to the man's first and second daughters. And today here the man was, a grandfather, but now a child again, humbled to tears by the grace of his old friend, who had just become one of the most famous people on the planet.

BEGINNINGS

"Bergoglio did not come from a laboratory," says Father Carlos Accaputo, one of the pope's most trusted advisers. "I think God has prepared him, throughout his entire pastoral ministry, for this moment."

This may be so. And it is manifestly true that every essential element of Pope Francis was present in the Padre Jorge that Argentines have known for decades. As Federico Wals, his former press aide, flatly says, "He has stayed himself. Francis is Padre Jorge, except in white."

Nonetheless, prior to the conclave of 2005—in which Bergoglio received the second most votes among the 115 cardinals until he insisted that they unite around Joseph Ratzinger, the soon-to-be-anointed Pope Benedict XVI—absolutely no one could have foreseen Padre Jorge's path to the papacy. He did not seek the job. Truthfully, he had not sought any of the leadership positions into which he was thrust. That he performed in those roles so impressively was a fact somewhat obscured by Jorge Mario Bergoglio's encompassing humbleness.

His was the first actual success story in a family tree of hardworking porteños, though in fact his forebears were from the northwest Italian region of Piedmont. In 1929 his grandparents immigrated to the new economic frontier of Argentina, bringing with them their son Mario Bergoglio, a recent college graduate with an accounting degree. At a parish in Buenos Aires in 1934, Mario met a young woman of Italian lineage, Regina Maria Sivori. They married a year later. On December 17, 1936, the Bergoglios welcomed the first of their five children, Jorge Mario.

The wall outside the house on 531 Membrillar in the bustling Flores district of Buenos Aires now bears a plaque with the inscription, "In this house lived Pope Francis." The Bergoglios' life was simple but for the most part without hardship. (The exception was when Jorge's mother became temporarily paralyzed following the birth of her fifth child. During that period, Jorge's mother taught him to cook for the family.) His accountant father insisted that his son appreciate the value of work at an early age,

In 1943, Pope Francis as a child (lower right) poses with his elementary school classmates from the Pedro Cervio school, Buenos Aires, Argentina.

and so at 13, Jorge took his first job in a hosiery factory next door to Mario's office. Like the other boys in Flores, he loved and played soccer, if not especially well.

Still, the pope who today emphasizes the Church's "maternal attitude"—its care and nurturing of all children—was especially influenced by the women of his youth. His mother routinely sat him beside the radio with her and listened to the opera broadcasts, inculcating in him an abiding love of music. His father's mother, a deeply spiritual woman, first stirred

his voracious appetite for literature by exposing him to Italian classics such as Alessandro Manzoni's *The Betrothed*. One of his early employers, at a chemical analysis laboratory in 1953, was a Paraguayan woman and Communist sympathizer. (She was later abducted and murdered in 1977, during the Argentine military dictatorship and while Jorge was serving as provincial of the Jesuits in Argentina.) Her insistence that Jorge do things the right way, without cutting any corners, would be reflected in his own teaching style.

As in his father's birthplace of Italy, to speak of religion in Argentina was to speak of the Catholic Church. The Bergoglios were reliable parishioners at San Jose de Flores—which is where, at the age of 17, Jorge dropped in one day for what he had intended to be a routine confession. But the priest that day—one he'd never met before—connected with him spiritually in a way that the boy had never experienced. He knew then that he was destined to enter the priesthood. Against the wishes of his mother, who wanted to see him attend the university, Jorge Bergoglio entered seminary school in 1957.

"He was one of the better students, but not the best," recalls Father Juan Carlos Scannone, who taught Bergoglio classical Greek. "He developed a severe illness, which turned out to be pneumonia, and they had to operate and take out a part of his lung. He endured the whole matter very well, though it caused him to speak with a lower voice, even today." (Decades later, certain adversaries of Cardinal Bergoglio within the Vatican would attempt to undermine his chances at becoming pope by spreading the false rumor that his lung was badly debilitated and would lead to a premature death.)

The following year, 21-year-old Jorge Bergoglio made a fateful decision: He would enter into the Society of Jesus. It was a slower path to the priesthood, one that would involve greater academic rigor as well as a deep engagement with his Jesuit brothers and with those in need throughout the world. Still, the spiritual order that the Basque priest St. Ignatius began 400 years earlier—inspired partly by another saint who would figure into Bergoglio's life, Francis of Assisi— spoke to the young man's twin dimensions: He was a cerebral introvert, and at the same time he was a porteño who craved the company of others.

On the campus of the Colegio Maximo de San Jose in San Miguel, just outside Buenos Aires, the philosophy student began to distinguish himself as a natural leader. His teacher and mentor Scannone notes that Bergoglio possessed not only a heightened "spiritual discernment" but also *"cintura politica"*— literally, a "political waist," the ability to maneuver strategically between opposing forces and to act as an intermediary in disputes. "You need both of these qualities in the Jesuit order," Scannone explains. "And I'm not suggesting 'political' in terms of ambition. This was a natural quality he had." It would also prove to be a necessary skill for a leading Argentine religious figure during the political tumult of the coming decades.

THE *MAESTRILLO*

Jorge Bergoglio's years as a teacher from 1964 to 1990 offer the first vivid portrait of the man who would be Pope Francis. Ironically, those same years have provided fodder for the pope's detractors as well as his admirers.

In 1964, as part of the Jesuit trajectory toward priesthood, his superiors assigned him to be a *maestrillo* (literally, a "little master," a kind of teaching student-priest) at the Institute of the Immaculate Conception in Santa Fe, Argentina. At that time, the prestigious Jesuit school took in primarily well-off boys, many of whom had not fared well in other educational settings. Most of the students lived on campus, far from their families, and thus somewhat at sea. They looked to the school's *maestrillos* as all-purpose paternal figures. "And all of them were so damned good as persons and teachers," says Martin Murphy, who attended the Institute from 1959 to 1965. "Sometimes you were very lonely, and the only guy you could look at as your friend was them."

Even among the impressive faculty there, Bergoglio set himself apart. "He was very down-to-earth, the person you wanted right next to you when you had a problem," remembers Yayo Grassi, a former student. "Somehow although each of us were assigned a different spiritual guide, he was basically the one for almost everyone. They loved to listen to him—and he himself was an extraordinary listener, with an amazing memory."

"Intellectually he was so stimulating," recalls Rogelio Pfirter, another student during that time. "He engaged us with theater, with works of great literature. And he treated us as grown-ups rather than students." His curriculum as a teacher of literature and psychology was anything but cookie-cutter; Pfirter remembers one morning of a Bergoglio class that was devoted entirely to American artistic interpretations of Jesus Christ's suffering on the cross. In 1965, Bergoglio somewhat audaciously persuaded the iconic Argentine man of letters Jorge Luis Borges—at that time 66 and much lionized, but also blind and resistant to travel—to board a bus bound for Santa Fe to meet some of his best writing students, hear them read their fiction, and critique their work. Some of those short stories would later be published in a book, *Cuentos Originales (Original Stories),* to which Borges himself contributed the introduction.

During his two-year tenure at Santa Fe, Bergoglio also exhibited two characteristics—strictness and leniency—that would be widely misunderstood throughout his life, all the more so because they appeared to contradict each other. His students knew him to be a personable instructor who nonetheless would not allow slacking off. "What distinguished him," says another former student, Jose Luis Lorenzatti, "was that he was dedicated to getting the full potential of every individual. He was demanding—but at the same time, he accompanied you throughout that process." Twenty years later, as a professor of theology and philosophy at his alma mater, Colegio Maximo, Bergoglio showed the same traits, according to former student Ramiro de la Serna: "As a professor, he was very *porteño,* using

jokes with double meanings, very picaresque. But at the same time, he was very strict, very demanding. He was close to the students, but he wasn't going to give us any extra points for that closeness."

This quality of high expectations is intrinsically Jesuit. The Italians refer to it as *il incontro,* the encounter, a rigorous communal engagement. But "demanding" can also be seen as "authoritarian" or, for that matter, "conservative"—terms that would later be appended to Jorge Bergoglio, and in ways not intended to flatter. Yet at the same time, the future Pope Francis could also be viewed as dangerously unorthodox—as a man insufficiently worshipful of the Church's rules—and thus liberal, even radical.

At Santa Fe, for example, the *maestrillo* taught his students the works of Pierre Teilhard de Chardin, a French Jesuit priest whose validation of evolution had made him persona non grata in the Catholic Church. At Colegio Maximo, the professor did not penalize a student for showing up to class wearing a habit that did not thoroughly cover his jeans. For that matter, while teaching at the Universidad de Salvador, Bergoglio had the reputation as a lenient priest. Former student Nicolas Kopistinski says: "When we would go to confession, you would always have to stand in line for a long time, because the priests would ask for every detail about your sins, then lecture you about it. Bergoglio, he was very quick: 'OK, here's your penance, here's your act of contrition, now out you go.' "

"He doesn't break the rules so much as make them more flexible, more commonsense," says Murphy, for whom Bergoglio bent the rules by officiating at his wedding, despite the fact that he was not the priest of that parish. That same informal, *porteño*-esque approach to his papacy would later endear Francis to millions—while at the same time inspiring considerable heartburn in the traditionalists inside the Vatican.

THROUGH THE UNREST

"Positions of power were given to him," observes Jorge Bergoglio's former student Lorenzatti, "because he always seemed to be the right person to do the job at that particular moment." His ascent in earnest began in 1973, when he became the provincial superior—effectively a governor—of the country's Jesuits. At 36, he was perhaps the youngest to hold such a post at that time throughout the entire Jesuit world. His six-year tenure coincided with emerging political instability and bloodshed in Argentina.

Bergoglio was never a political animal per se. But he was an avid news reader and spoke often of Argentina's vicissitudes. The Jesuit regarded his mother country, with its great natural resources, as one of tragically unfulfilled potential. "According to the Italians," he told writers Francesca Ambrogetti and Sergio Rubin, "you throw a seed in the street in Argentina and a plant springs up." He recited to the same writers a mordant joke in which several ambassadors from other countries complain to God that he had given Argentina too much. God's reply: "Yes, but I also gave them Argentines."

Bergoglio had come of age during the era of Juan Perón, and his own leadership style would in some ways borrow from the crafty president, who, along with

The bedroom where the pontiff lived while studying for the priesthood at the Colegio Maximo San Miguel conveys the simple life for which he is known.

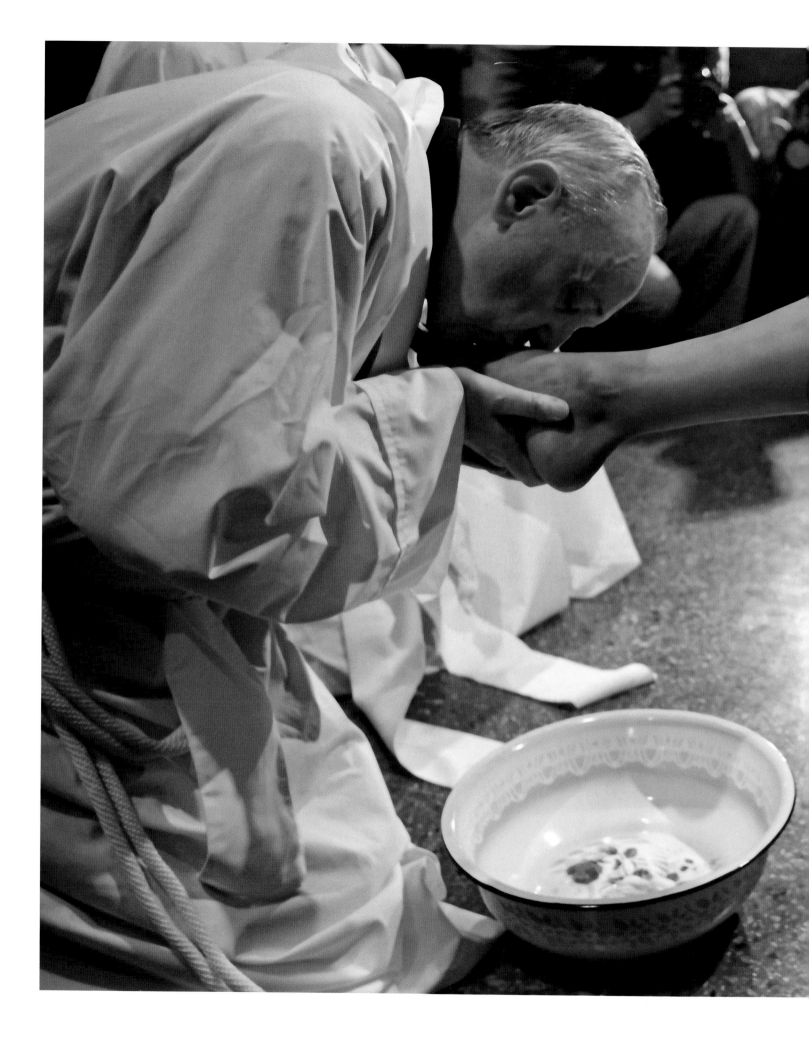

his wife Eva, skillfully knitted together an unlikely coalition that included labor, military leaders, women (to whom Perón had extended suffrage), and the Catholic Church. But the Church denounced Perón for legalizing divorce, and in 1955 the Vatican formally excommunicated him. A military junta chased Perón out of power that same year; he returned to the presidency in 1973, only to die in office a year later. His second wife, Isabel, succeeded him. She was pushed out of office in 1976 following a second military coup, one that would usher in a seven-year era of repression and state-sponsored assassination often referred to as the dirty war.

As provincial superior, Jorge Bergoglio was responsible for assigning priests to various posts throughout the country and abroad. The Society of Jesus faced a host of financial and institutional challenges. In addition, the liberation theology movement—in which the Church was seen as a vehicle to address social injustice—was gaining traction throughout Latin America, creating divisions that were not always collegial. Characteristically, Bergoglio's views acted as a bridge: He subscribed to a *teologia del pueblo,* or theology of the people, a concept his former teacher Scannone developed. As Dr. Francisco Pinon, the rector of the Universidad de Congreso, who held that same position at the Universidad de Salvador while Bergoglio was provincial, puts it: "He subscribed fully to liberation theology's view of the Church as the church of the poor, but he left aside Marxism. The Marxists weren't concerned about the poor the way Jesus was."

Decades later, the American conservative commentator Rush Limbaugh would express horror at the "pure Marxism coming out of the mouth of the pope."

The latter would in turn declare that caring about the poor was "not an invention of Communism . . . Is it pauperism? No. It is the Gospel." Dr. Pinon, for his part, scoffs at such criticism: "It's nonsense. There are thousands of differences between him and the Communists. For example, the belief in freedom. For another, the rejection of violence. I've never understood this!"

What the provincial superior did champion were *callejeros*—the street priests who worked extensively in the city's numerous *villas,* or shantytowns. Many such priests happened to embrace liberation theology. Says Scannone, "In fact, if you talked about liberation theology, you were considered a Communist by the military." During Bergoglio's tenure, the Catholic Church had essentially adopted a see-no-evil attitude toward (and, at times, a malignant complicity with) the military dictatorship, much as it had during Juan Perón's program of providing safe haven to Nazi war criminals. When numerous Argentine priests were labeled enemies of the state and thereafter targeted for harassment or worse, the Church did not condemn the government with the vehemence that it had shown the Peronistas for legalizing divorce and prostitution. As a key member of the Jesuit hierarchy, Jorge Bergoglio would be accused of complicity—particularly in the navy's abduction and torture in 1976 of two well-known Argentine Jesuit *callejeros,* Orlando Yorio and Franz Jalics.

Several of the future pope's contemporaries forcefully reject the claim that Provincial Bergoglio stood by idly while fellow Jesuit priests like Yorio and Jalics were swept up in the military's dragnet. Pinon and Scannone are among those who testify that Bergoglio went to great lengths to ferry priests out of danger while at the

Bishop Bergoglio visits the Villa 21-24 slum in 1998. "Padre Jorge" long recruited priests to work in the slums.

same time negotiating with the military for the release of Yorio and Jalics. (Both were deposited in a desert five months after their abduction. Shortly after Bergoglio became pope, Jalics released a statement absolving the former provincial of blame.) Says Pinon, "I heard him say it: Being a Christian involves danger. If you're not willing to risk upsetting the authorities, then you're not getting close enough to the people."

None of this is to suggest that Bergoglio was a flawless provincial superior. As he told Ambrogetti and Rubin, "I had to learn from my errors along the way because, to tell you the truth, I made hundreds of errors." He elaborated to Antonio Spadaro, editor in chief of *La Civiltà Cattolica:* "My authoritarian and quick manner of making decisions led me to have serious problems and to be accused of being ultraconservative."

Still, whatever bullheadedness he exhibited as provincial does not seem to be what forced him out of favor with his Jesuit superiors. Rather, it was the strong influence he wielded in Jesuit academia—first as rector of Colegio Maximo in 1980–86, and then in 1987 as a teacher at the Colegio del Salvador—that unnerved the Jesuit powers whose vision of theology did not dovetail with Bergoglio's.

"He had so much influence with the students," says Scannone, "that in my opinion they felt the need to put him away." And so in 1990 Jorge Bergoglio was ostracized by his superiors, banished to serve as a confessor in Córdoba, Argentina's second largest city behind Buenos Aires, set in the country's central region nearly 500 miles from the nation's capital. For two years he remained in exile. Then, seemingly out of nowhere,

Bergoglio the *callejero* practiced
what he preached . . .

the Archbishop of Buenos Aires, Cardinal Antonio Quarracino, put in a good word to the Vatican about the Jesuit he referred to as *el santito* (the little saint). On May 20, 1992, Pope John Paul II awarded Bergoglio the title of auxiliary bishop for the Archdiocese of Buenos Aires.

The *porteño* was coming home.

REACHING NEW HEIGHTS—
AND PERIPHERIES

Jorge Bergoglio's assumption of the Buenos Aires archdiocese—rising from auxiliary bishop in 1992 to archbishop in 1998 following Quarracino's death, and then to cardinal in 2001—came at a time when the credibility of the Catholic Church in Argentina was slowly rebounding from its nadir in the 1980s. Its unseemly relationship with the military dictatorship, combined with financial scandals and grotesque episodes of pedophilia within the priesthood (most notably Father Julio Cesar Grassi, whom Bergoglio and other Church officials defended even after Grassi was convicted of child molestation), made the Church a constant target of media ridicule. Nonetheless, as Bergoglio biographer Austen Ivereigh notes, "[a Gallup poll] put the Church first of institutions that Argentines most trusted, with politicians and judiciary at the bottom." The country was wracked by economic turmoil, which in 2001 triggered riots and, subsequently, Fernando de la Rúa's abdication of the presidency.

Archbishop Bergoglio asserted himself as a community leader, according to Buenos Aires Evangelical minister Juan Pablo Bongarra: "During that time of crisis, Bergoglio held meetings with key people from unions, big businesses, the spiritual community, and academia to try to assist the government. He played an important role in trying to unite people and maintain peace."

In the meantime, Bergoglio also catalyzed a quiet revolution within the Church—emphasizing, as Pope Francis later would, its obligation to *la periferia*, the downtrodden periphery of the city. "In those times, there were ten priests assigned to the *villas*," recalls Father José di Paola, more commonly known as Padre Pepe, one of the country's most dedicated shantytown priests. "Within three or four years after Bergoglio became archbishop, the number of us in the *villas* had grown to 22. This wasn't something we were used to."

But, Padre Pepe adds, Bergoglio the *callejero* practiced what he preached: "When he chose his moments to give a public speech, he didn't do so at a cathedral. Instead, he'd go to Plaza Constitución"—a shabby nexus of drug dealing and prostitution—"or in the humble neighborhoods. In his view, the center wasn't the city. The center was the people for whom there's no hope in the city. And that's where he would go."

He went to the *villas* not only as a moral imperative but also as a matter of personal affinity. "He felt more comfortable with those who have less," says former press aide Federico Wals. "He felt their faith was deeper than those who are fortunate." Padre Pepe would recall the only time he ever saw the Archbishop of Buenos Aires display great emotion. It was when Bergoglio showed up to a *villa* by bus. Upon arriving, one of the residents, a construction worker, proclaimed to the rest that he had seen this bishop riding in the back of the

As cardinal, Pope Francis greets parishioners in Buenos Aires during the celebration of St. Cajetan, the patron saint of bread and work.

bus with him and the other *porteños,* that he was truly one of them. "You could see his eyes watering," says the shantytown priest.

Even those who had criticized Bergoglio for his passivity during the "dirty war" could never find fault in his lifestyle, which was utterly devoid of ostentation. He never wore gaudy jewelry. He did not dine at fancy restaurants, though as a man of *piemontese* (Italian Piedmont) roots, he harbored a weakness for gnocchi. During Christmastime, his office was flooded with "gifts from the best shops in Buenos Aires," recalls

Wals. "Calvin Klein shirts, perfumes, chocolates, champagne. And automatically he dispersed them throughout the office. He kept nothing for himself. Nothing." Though Bergoglio knew how to drive, he preferred to commute by bus or on the city subway's A line—a radical departure from most bishops, who typically had chauffeurs. This endeared him to the younger clerics.

They also admired his disarming frankness. During a Holy Thursday in 2008, the archbishop showed up at a hospital to wash the feet of several terminally ill children. Those present braced themselves for the usual pious bromides: *God loves you . . . with prayer there is hope . . . heaven awaits . . .* Instead, Jorge Bergoglio said, "I really don't understand why God allows his angels to suffer like this. I suffer with you." The archbishop then spoke to the dying children, washed their feet, greeted the medical staff, and walked out the hospital door, to the nearest bus stop.

A ROME-BOUND SHEPHERD

On June 19, 2006, Jorge Bergoglio gave the public the first vivid glimpse of the future Pope Francis. The occasion was an ecumenical gathering of 7,000 Catholics and Evangelical Christians inside an arena at Luna Park, in eastern Buenos Aires, Argentina. From the stage, a pastor called for the Archbishop of Buenos Aires to come up and say a few words. The audience reacted with surprise, because the man striding to the platform had been sitting in the back of the arena all this time, for hours, like no one of importance. He was wearing not the red garb of the cardinal that he was but instead the black raiment of the simple parish priest that he had once been, nearly a half century ago.

Bergoglio stood behind the microphone and spoke—quietly at first, though with steady nerves. He had no notes. In truth, he didn't have all that much to say. The speech was more about what he did not say. The archbishop said nothing about the sanctity of Catholic doctrine. He made no reference to the Catholic Church's governing body, the Vatican, which in a year would state explicitly what it had for centuries promulgated implicitly: namely, that there is but "one church," the Catholic Church, while all other churches are mere "communities." Nor did Bergoglio mention the days when he regarded the Evangelical movement in the dismissive way many Catholic priests did, as an *escuela de samba*—an unserious happening akin to a Brazilian samba dance.

Instead, the most powerful Argentine in the Catholic Church proclaimed that no such distinctions matter to God. "How nice," Bergoglio said, "that brothers are united, that brothers speak together. How nice to see that no one negotiates his history on the path to faith—that we are diverse, but that we want to be, and are already beginning to be, a reconciled diversity." Hands outstretched, his face suddenly elastic and his voice quavering with passion, he called out to God: "Father, we are divided—unite us!"

Those present who knew Jorge Bergoglio were astonished, since his implacable expression had previously earned him nicknames like Mona Lisa and Carucha (for his bulldog-like jaws). But what most remember about that day occurred immediately after Bergoglio stopped talking. He dropped slowly to his knees, onstage—a plea for the 7,000 attendees, Catholics and Evangelicals alike, to pray for him. And after a startled pause, they did so, an Evangelical minister leading them. The image of the Archbishop of Buenos Aires kneeling before men of lesser status, in a posture of supplication at once meek and awesome, would, within hours, make every front page in Argentina. Among the publications that carried the photograph was *Cabildo*, a conservative online journal. The headline accompanying the story featured a jarring noun: *Apostasia*. The Archbishop of Buenos Aires as apostate, a traitor of one's religion.

Just a year earlier, in 2005 following Pope John Paul II's death, several members of the international press—the so-called *Vaticanisti*—had shown up in Buenos Aires and begun asking questions of friends and colleagues about Cardinal Bergoglio. Rumors were circulating that some viewed him as a possible successor—as *papabile,* or pope-worthy. Bergoglio's friends were stunned to hear such talk. For all their reverence for the man, it was hard to imagine the austere Bergoglio as a white-cloaked international

The bemused press watched the
new cardinal shamble in, having arrived
by public transport ...

figure. And though he was viewed as an important leader within Latin America's Catholic community, Bergoglio had not sought to involve himself in the Vatican's affairs. Whenever he spoke of Rome, it was with tart disapproval.

This was not to say that Bergoglio was wholly indifferent to the Church's leadership. In April 2001, just two months after John Paul II had appointed him cardinal, Bergoglio was invited to attend a gathering of Argentina's foreign correspondents. The bemused press watched the new cardinal shamble in, having arrived by public transport, carrying a beaten black satchel. But he caught their attention when the question was asked, "What should the profile of the next pope be?" Bergoglio answered immediately with a single word: "*Pastor.*" A shepherd.

As it happened, Bergoglio was the runner-up recipient of votes during the first three rounds of balloting in the April 2005 conclave. Only when the Argentine sent signals of his reluctance to be a part of protracted electoral infighting did the front-runner, Joseph Ratzinger—widely seen as an ideological doppelgänger of John Paul II, and thus the safe bet—achieve the two-thirds majority needed to win and thereby become Pope Benedict XVI.

Thereafter Bergoglio's influence grew, particularly in Latin America. There was talk of making him Pope Benedict's secretary of state. Bergoglio recoiled at the thought. As he told Reuters, "I shall die if I go to the Curia."

In 2010, the Institute of the Immaculate Conception's class of 1965 convened in Buenos Aires for a reunion and persuaded their former teacher Padre Jorge to join them. They met in a church, where the Archbishop of Buenos Aires presided over Mass with his ex-students and their spouses. Then it was just the classmates and their *maestrillo.* They shared with him their personal trajectories, asked for advice, and recited their beloved memories from 45 years ago. Though polite as always, Bergoglio seemed inattentive—"very preoccupied, in another place, not with us," recalls former student Murphy.

It had been a trying year. The federal government had demanded that he testify in court about his role in the mistreatment of priests by the military during the 1970s. He had also been embroiled that same year in protesting the new law that made Argentina the first Latin American country to legalize same-sex marriage. Bergoglio's weariness was palpable. Against their protestations, he told his former students that he was "closing chapters," "tying up loose ends." In December he would be 74. He intended to submit his resignation to the Vatican the following year, as was required of all cardinals who reached the age of 75.

Bergoglio did make one telling comment to the gathering. He observed that the Catholic Church, beset by sex and financial scandals, was in a state of chaos. He compared its current malaise to the fall of the Roman Empire. The Church would have to change, he told them. But Jorge Bergoglio showed no interest in spearheading it.

In late January 2013, his longtime adviser Carlos Accaputo met with Cardinal Bergoglio in his office for

Residents of the Villa 21-24 slum pray in the Virgin of Caacupé chapel to celebrate Padre Jorge's election as pope. He used to give Mass in this very chapel.

one of their regular chats about the state of the archdiocese, which evolved into a more sweeping discussion about the state of the Church. Marveling yet again at the archbishop's simple but acute observations, he found himself blurting out, "Jorge, you're going to be the next pope."

Bergoglio quickly waved him off. "I was close in 2005," he said. "But I'm old. There are plenty of younger candidates."

Accaputo persisted. "Jorge," he said, "God gave you a unique gift—the ability to cut through all the nonsense and see reality for what it is. So you say you're old. Think of what you could do in four years' time. You could put the Church back on the right path."

Bergoglio chuckled and said, "Let's go," signaling that the conversation had come to an end.

Eleven days later, on February 11, 2013, Pope Benedict stunned the world by submitting a letter to

In the days before his departure, he spoke to no one about what he thought would transpire on March 12 . . .

the Vatican that contained words no one had foreseen: "I have come to the certainty that my strengths, due to an advanced age, are no longer suited to an adequate exercise of the Petrine ministry . . ."

Jorge Mario Bergoglio booked his ticket to Rome. In the days before his departure, he spoke to no one about what he thought would transpire on March 12, when he and 114 other cardinals would be sequestered inside the Sistine Chapel for as long as it took the conclave to agree upon Pope Benedict's successor. Among the *Vaticanisti*—who covered these rare electoral events with the unsentimental fervor of Vegas oddsmakers—speculation focused on several candidates, none of them Bergoglio. The Vatican's mind-set, they noted, was habitually Eurocentric. That meant the front-runner was surely Angelo Scola, the Archbishop of Milan.

If the conclave's end was to seek a change but not too great a change, the obvious candidate was the Archbishop of São Paulo, Brazil, Odilo Pedro Scherer: He would be the first Latino pope, but one with many years of experience in the Curia. If, on the other hand, the cardinals sought to generate an earthquake, they could name Ghana cardinal Peter Turkson as the papacy's first African in more than a thousand years. The reality was that there was no heir apparent as there had been in 2005. But until the days preceding the conclave, Bergoglio as pope was a notion almost no one held.

Save perhaps one. "The night before Bergoglio left for Rome," recalls Federico Wals, "he called me into his office and we stayed there late, preparing the last details of the flight. But really, he just wanted to talk to me. It was very strange. He had left us with all letters finished, the money in order, everything in perfect shape."

The archbishop had been a father figure to his 27-year-old press aide—whom he hired in 2007, fresh out of college, jobless and with a pregnant wife, and with absolutely no experience in media affairs. But the young man came to Bergoglio with a recommendation that he was competent and trustworthy. A few months after Wals began work, Cardinal Bergoglio paid a visit to his house to introduce himself to the aide's wife and infant daughter. Maria Wals was a devout Catholic, and the prospect of meeting such an eminence left her tongue-tied. Bergoglio immediately put her at ease. "Tell me, Maria, do you two fight and throw plates at each other?" he asked with a sly smile. When she confessed that they did at times quarrel, Bergoglio replied, "Thank God you told me that. If you'd said otherwise, I wouldn't have believed you. It's normal to fight. A couple that doesn't fight has no future together. What's important is to make up after."

So it was not altogether strange for Bergoglio to be talking to his staffer as he would a son. Still, that evening the archbishop proceeded to offer unsolicited advice about the young man's future—work, money, family—in a way that he had never done before. At the time, but even more so later, Federico Wals could not help thinking that these were the words, he now says, of "someone who knew that maybe he would be leaving for good."

FAMILIES
and
FRANCIS

✠

Family, the foundation of coexistence,
is at the heart of continuing faith
according to Pope Francis.
Encouraging love, lifelong commitment,
and shared truths, the pope advocates
the family's essentiality to humankind's
survival. And in turn, families—
newlywed and generation-spanning—
look to Pope Francis for guidance.

Pages 102–103: Parents hold their babies over a barricade to receive the pope's blessing.

Previous pages: Newlywed couples (or *sposi novelli*) in wedding dresses and suits line up to receive the pope's blessing as tears flow freely.

Below: A bride holds her wedding bands out for Pope Francis to bless.

Above: Newlyweds wait to meet the pope. The Church celebrates marriage, one of the seven sacraments.

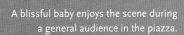

The family is where
we are formed as
people. Every family is
a brick in the building
of society.

POPE FRANCIS

Always at the ready with an easy laugh, Pope Francis connects with newlyweds during a general audience.

Although the life of a person
is a land full of thorns and weeds,
there is always a space in which
the good seed can grow.

POPE FRANCIS

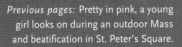

People begin arriving early in the morning
for the mid-morning papal audience.
At times the piazza takes on
the feel of an outdoor rock concert.

Take care of your
family life, giving your
children and loved ones
not just money, but
most of all your time,
attention and love.

POPE FRANCIS

Previous pages and opposite: Pope Francis
often shares thoughts with couples. Family
is a focus of his ministry, and addressing
modern mores, he has remarked, "In our day,
marriage and the family" are in crisis.

I ask you to be revolutionaries,
to swim against the tide;
yes, I am asking you to rebel
against this culture that
sees everything as temporary
and that ultimately believes
that you are incapable
of responsibility, that you are
incapable of true love.

POPE FRANCIS

There seems to be something universal about
holding up children for the pope to see. Such an
up-close visit is a once-in-a-lifetime event for many.

We must restore hope to
young people, help the
old, be open to the future,
spread love. Be poor
among the poor. We need
to include the excluded
and preach peace.

POPE FRANCIS

Previous pages: The inspector general of the Gendarme Corps of Vatican City holds up a young boy, who doesn't seem quite sure how he feels to be blessed by the pope.

Below: An embrace and an expression of joy come naturally for this bride, when in the presence of Pope Francis.

Above: Brides get to wear their wedding dresses twice, once for the wedding and again for the papal audience.

Following pages: The pope belongs in this world, and the world is moved by him.

THE
TRADITION
OF THE VATICAN

Pages 134–135: A ceremony marking the end of the command of the 34th head of the Pontifical Swiss Guard, Daniel Anrig, displays the pomp and ritual of the Vatican.

A composite image of the interior of St. Peter's Basilica presents the grandeur of Michelangelo's dome and Bernini's baldachin, or canopy. A church has stood on this site since the time of the Roman emperor Constantine.

One morning in 2014 immediately following Wednesday Mass, Pope Francis presided over a smaller Mass service in Santa Marta. Among the group was his old friend, the Franciscan priest Ramiro de la Serna, who runs a youth ministry just outside Buenos Aires. The pope knew that de la Serna would be among the congregants but nonetheless feigned surprise as they greeted each other. "Ramiro! What are you doing here?" Francis declared in mock horror. "Don't be caught by the Romans! Go back to Argentina and do your good works with the young people!" • Father de la Serna laughed. He understood well the sentiment beneath the pope's wisecrack. For all of its majesty, Vatican City remained an imperfect model of spiritual purity. It is a city behind walls, and thus antithetical to the man who, as Archbishop of Buenos Aires, once said to a friend as they strolled together past the president's residence, Casa

Pope Francis has simultaneously abided by and challenged the Vatican's ancient traditions.

Rosada: "How can they know what the common people want when they build a fence around themselves?"

Today Pope Francis has simultaneously abided by and challenged the Vatican's ancient traditions. He lives behind the city's walls. But he has eschewed the quarters that were built in the 16th century expressly for the private use of popes: the Apostolic Palace, as grand and cavernous as the name implies. The palace includes the Vatican Museums and a host of administrative offices—the powerful Secretariat of State among them—as well as a number of papal apartments.

In a richly symbolic move, Francis has instead chosen to live in Santa Marta. It is one of the newest structures in Vatican City, built in 1996 at the directive of Pope John Paul II, who desired a guesthouse for the more than 100 cardinals who would gather as a conclave to elect future popes. The five-story building with its more than 120 guest rooms sits on the grounds where, a century earlier, the hospice of Santa Marta tended to the poor and took in wayfaring pilgrims. Though the papal apartment awaiting Francis in the Apostolic Palace was not lavish in furnishings, its sheer size overwhelmed him. His reaction to it, he told friends, was, "What would I do in such a place?"

By contrast, Suite 201 is a two-room residence comprising about 160 square feet. He takes his meals in the Jesuit manner: in the guesthouse dining room, alongside building employees and visiting clergy. When Francis learned that his dining napkin was being replaced at every meal, he protested, saying that this was wasteful. Thereafter the pope's napkin is replaced only a handful of times per week.

"For me, it was quite a surprise when he decided not to live in the papal apartment, but instead to be in Santa Marta," says the longtime Vatican communications director Father Federico Lombardi. "It is one thing to agree with the philosophy of Francis's lifestyle, which I do. But to be so clear and say, 'No, I will change this aspect'—for me, it was something very courageous."

INSIDE THE CITY WALLS

Like any institution, the Vatican is both impregnable and frail, unreceptive to change and suspicious of those who would bring it. Since the 14th century, the Catholic epicenter has resided as a 110-acre walled city-state within central Rome. Traditionally, the world has come to the Vatican, rather than the other way around. It has long been one of Europe's predominant tourist meccas, particularly as a repository of Christianity's episodic 2,000-year history.

The obelisk brought from Egypt to Rome around A.D. 40 as a centerpiece of Caligula's circus sits today in the heart of St. Peter's Square. Traces also exist of Caligula's horse-racing track in the Vatican valley, which was reportedly later used by his nephew Nero as the site of Christian executions—including, some documents say, St. Peter (by crucifixion) and St. Paul (by decapitation). An entire necropolis—said to be full of Roman Christians who wished to be buried near Peter—was discovered directly beneath St. Peter's Basilica in the 1940s and is viewable today. Fragments of the first basilica of the emperor Constantine, who in A.D. 313 decreed an end to the persecution of Christians, also remain.

Ushers wait in an antechamber of the Apostolic Palace for the end of a papal audience with the president of Austria, Heinz Fischer.

But three particular things primarily account for the Vatican's seven million annual visitors. One is St. Peter's great basilica, with its sweeping marble naves and porticoes lined with Renaissance art. Crowned by Michelangelo's gigantic dome, it rivals the Colosseum as the most important visual reference point in Rome. Adjacent to the basilica are the Vatican Museums (receiving an average of 25,000 visitors daily). The most famous of these is the traditional domestic place of papal worship (and the place where popes are elected by the conclave): the Sistine Chapel. Named after Sixtus IV, the pope who commissioned it, the chapel features a staggering compression of Renaissance art—again, the most iconic being the ceiling Michelangelo painted,

which includes "The Creation of Adam." Last but hardly least as a tourist attraction is the pope himself, who presides over Wednesday Mass on the basilica steps. Tens of thousands of spectators weekly bunch along elegant St. Peter's Square, which was designed in the 17th century for precisely that purpose.

The machinations of Vatican politics notwithstanding, and despite the vulgarities associated with any tourist mecca, the Vatican constitutes sacred ground for the planet's 1.2 billion Catholics. But Vatican City is also just as its designation implies: a territorial entity. International law has recognized its sovereignty since 1929, when the papacy and Italy (ruled at the time by Benito Mussolini) signed the Lateran Pacts. The city

is also distinct from the ecclesiastical jurisdiction within its perimeters, known as the Holy See.

It is a nation of manifest peculiarities. No other country has been designated in its entirety a UNESCO World Heritage site. A gated community in every sense of the phrase, Vatican City's entrances close at midnight. Parents and siblings are the only guests permitted to stay overnight in the residences. An understood dress code of covered knees, arms, and necklines prevails. (Sunbathing is prohibited.) So does an almost monastic quietude. Divorce in Vatican City is extremely rare. Security is tight and monitoring is intense, though there is no prison in which to confine offenders. (Vatican City has been said to have the highest crime rate per capita of any nation in the world, as well as the highest alcohol consumption of any country. But the city's tiny population skews these statistics, making these distinctions less meaningful, if somewhat bemusing.)

Its most important inhabitant, the pope, has been protected since 1506 by a nattily attired yet fierce (i.e., trained in martial arts and firearms expertise) all-Swiss mercenary force known as the Pontifical Swiss Guard. As the name suggests, the 110 or so members of the guard are all Swiss citizens. Otherwise, three-fourths of Vatican City's approximately 800 residents are clergy from around the world. Only 450 of them hold Vatican citizenship. (And

Cardinal Timothy Dolan, archbishop of the Archdiocese of New York, speaks with another cardinal during the Synod on the Family.

No other country has been designated in its entirety a UNESCO World Heritage site.

only 30 of the latter are women.) Even fewer actually live within the city's walls: The scarce housing is strictly limited to a lucky 13 or so families. These include certain members of the Swiss Guard, the Holy See's electrician and head gardener, and—in the monastery known as Mater Ecclesiae—the retired Pope Benedict XVI.

Population-wise, it is fairly congested compared with, say, the Pitcairn Islands, with its approximately 50 residents. In terms of sheer landmass, however, Vatican City is the smallest country in the world by a long shot—smaller than Manhattan, smaller even than Central Park. Despite its sovereign status, no passport stamps are issued in Vatican City.

But beyond these anomalous characteristics, the city functions more or less in the manner of any other self-contained territorial body. Since gaining independence in 1929, it has flown its own flag, distinguished by St. Peter's crossed keys, which symbolize the entrance to heaven. It has both a primary language (Italian) and an "official" if seldom-used one (Latin). The Gendarmerie Corps—consisting largely of former Italian officers and currently staffed by a bald, intense former Italian secret service agent named Domenico Giani—handles all security, border enforcement, and investigative matters. Its 130 or so members have managed these duties since 1970, when Pope Paul VI dissolved all but the Swiss Guard division of the Vatican's military corps as part of a series of institutional reforms. The Vatican's international press corps, or *Vaticanisti,* monitors the institution's vagaries with the gimlet-eyed skepticism of city hall reporters.

The city's governing structure—operating parallel to the Roman Curia, which oversees the affairs of the Catholic Church under the pope's leadership—includes a local governorate, a diplomatic division, a judicial branch (including an appellate and Supreme Court), a Department of Utilities, a Department of Health and Welfare, a Department of Goods and Services (to oversee commercial activity), and a kind of all-purpose Department of Pontifical Villas (which in addition to maintaining the palaces and gardens also administers the city's various agricultural and animal husbandry activities, as well as its parking garage). And inconspicuously wedged inside the lovely 16th-century Belvedere Courtyard, which links the ancient pontifical palace with the villa built for Pope Innocent VIII, is another standard institutional feature: the Vatican City fire station, complete with its own blue Fiat fire trucks.

And, well known to the scandal-conscious world is the Institute for the Works of Religion, also known as the Vatican Bank. *Forbes* in 2012 termed it "the most secret bank in the world." Though Vatican City subsists on a steady stream of tourist dollars—book sales, museum admission fees, souvenirs—its bank holds deposits from religious entities around the world, and its books have, at least until the time of Pope Francis, been kept in mists of obscurity. The bank's employees have often been individuals more notable for their connections than for their acumen, a hard reality that applies throughout Vatican City. As veteran Reuters reporter Philip Pullella observes, "Typically the people put into jobs like the bank are Italian relatives of cardinals, people that can be depended on to keep everyone in the Vatican happy. It's not quite a sinecure, but still: salary, no taxes, VAT-free grocery store. It's like dying and going to heaven. Nobody quits."

Items are prepared for a Holy Mass in the Papal Sacristy, next to the Sistine Chapel.

Vatican City has its own railway, servicing the train that delivers duty-free goods once a week. It has as well a heliport (though no airplane runway) for the pope's use. In keeping with sovereign territories everywhere, it also has its own postal service, and the Philatelic and Numismatic Office has been printing and selling commemorative Vatican City stamps since 1852. The city also mints its own euro coins, though in very limited quantity. On July 1, 1861, following the establishment of the Kingdom of Italy, the Vatican printed the first edition of its local paper, *L'Osservatore Romano*, which today remains in daily circulation and is laudably less propagandistic than in its earlier years. Since 1931, Vatican City has transmitted the Catholic Church's

message to the outside world via Radio Vaticana. Its production studio today sits a stone's throw from the Tiber River and broadcasts programs to every continent, in 39 languages. In 1983, the media-savvy Pope John Paul II launched the Vatican Television Center, which has since been chiefly responsible for broadcasting images of the pope around the world.

The city also has the pedestrian features of a typical municipality. There is a grocery store as well as a gas station. (Owing to the lack of sales taxes within Vatican City, both are lower in cost and thus much frequented. The city commissary, which offers duty-free shopping on luxury brands like Prada and Armani, is also highly popular.) A small medical clinic serves the

Pages 144–145: Guards and support staff
fill a Vatican hallway during a meeting
between the pope and the president of Malta.

community, though there is no hospital, and thus no births within the city walls. And in October 2013, Pope Francis introduced an innovation to the city: its own cricket team, consisting primarily of young seminarians from the cricket-loving countries of India, Pakistan, Sri Lanka, and England. (In September 2014, the St. Peter's Cricket Club went on tour to play a succession of matches, from which the proceeds were donated to various charities. The upstarts from Vatican City surprised many by winning two of its five matches—but unsurprisingly, the Anglican Church team thrashed them in the finale.)

THE POPE AND THE VATICAN

Throughout history, the Vatican and its city have been animated—and ultimately defined by—its leader. The first pope, the originator of the Catholic Church, is understood to be the apostle St. Peter—to whom Jesus said, according to Scripture (Matthew 16:18), "And I tell you that you are Peter, and on this rock I will build my church, and the gates of Hades will not overcome it." The term "Catholic" (from the Greek adjective *katholikos,* which means "worldwide" or "universal") does not appear in conjunction with "church" until well after Peter's death by crucifixion in A.D. 64. Likewise "pope" (from the Greek *pappas,* or "father") referred generally to all bishops for several centuries. Nonetheless, all popes are said to be descendants of Peter, and as such have often been buried in proximity to his tomb. (John Paul II is entombed less than a hundred feet from Peter.)

The Vatican's history is no less murky than any culture of ancient origins, though it benefits from well-preserved texts. It apparently took nearly 500 years before the penning of the *Liber Pontificalis,* or papal biography, commenced. Peter's successor as Bishop of Rome, St. Linus, was a Tuscan who appointed the

first 15 bishops and also decreed that women should cover their heads when attending church (a Catholic tradition that remained in effect through the beginning of the 20th century). Though texts assert that Linus was martyred circa 78—during the reign of Vespasian, builder of the Colosseum—nothing else about his death is recorded. Thus begins the shrouded and much debated evolution of the Catholic Church.

Some facts are easy enough to determine. For example, papal history reflects that there has been only one Peter—and now, a single Pope Francis. Likely there will not be another pope who takes the name Dionysius, as did the man whose nine-year reign (A.D. 260–268) was not marked by drunken revelry, as the moniker would suggest, but instead by prudent administration. In all probability the Church will, however, see more Gregorys (16 as of 2015) and Johns (21 as of the same year).

One can also trace papal origins with reasonable certainty. Fully 217 of history's 266 popes are of Italian nationality. After the only Dutch pope, Hadrian VI, died in 1523, an unbroken succession of Italian-born popes continued until Poland's Karol Józef Wojtyla became John Paul II in 1978, some four centuries later. That trend would now appear reversed, the last three popes hailing from outside Italy. In particular, the election for the first time of a Latin American may well make possible the election of future popes from elsewhere in the Americas, or for that matter, from Africa. (The last of three African popes, Gelasius I, served from 492 until 496.)

Less clear is how the Church cohered, both organizationally and doctrinally, over the centuries. It appears that priests first became answerable to the Bishop of Rome under Pius I (142–155), who also decreed that Easter be observed exclusively on Sundays. The vow of celibacy in the priesthood evidently was not enforced in the earlier years, given that several popes seem to have been married, starting with Peter himself. Some were sons of priests, such as Innocent I, who is said to be the offspring of Pope Anastasius. It was during Innocent's papacy that the Visigoths invaded Rome in 410, marking the first time in eight centuries that the great city was sacked. In what would begin a very mixed record of papal diplomacy, Innocent went to great lengths to pacify the Visigoths, including by allowing private pagan rituals. Four decades later, Pope Leo I showed considerably more fortitude, managing to persuade Attila the Hun to desist from invading Italy entirely.

Though the emperor Constantine I erected a papal residency at the Lateran Palace after decreeing an end to the Christian persecution in the early fourth century, Pope Symmachus foreshadowed a later tradition by choosing to live in a smaller palace next to the basilica that Constantine had built to honor St. Peter. It was then that the physical concept of a Vatican began to take shape. As the Roman Empire's decline continued into the ninth century, Pope Leo IV oversaw the construction of walls to protect the basilica from invading barbarians.

In truth, the Church needed protection at least as much from its leaders. The years following Leo IV saw a ghastly deterioration in papal integrity. There was Stephen VI, who in 897 dug up the corpse of his predecessor, Pope Formosus, and tried him for being unworthy of the office. There was Sergius III (904–911), the first pope to wear a crown—a tradition that would last until 1963—and was said to have presided over a morally vacant "pornocracy." There was John XII (955–964), a secular prince with the lifestyle to match, who fittingly died during an act of adultery. And there was Benedict IX (1032–1044), the Nero-like 20-year-old boy pope who at one point sold his papacy to the highest bidder.

A single outstanding leader of the Church loomed from this dreary litany: Gregory VII (1073–1085), who like his namesake Gregory the Great instituted a host of consequential reforms: the enforcement of celibacy, the abolition of the clergy-selling practice known as simony,

the formalization of an electoral conclave, and a decree that the word "pope" would apply only to the Bishop of Rome among them. By the time of Gregory VII's papacy, the East-West schism in the Catholic Church had just occurred over long-running theological disagreements. That split between Constantinople (Eastern Orthodox) and the Vatican (Roman Catholic) would remain even after the Ecumenical Patriarch of Constantinople Athenagoras I and Pope Paul VI formally nullified the 1054 decree that gave rise to the divide.

Seeking to regain some of the territory the Church lost during the Muslim conquests of the seventh century, Pope Urban II in 1095 led troops into the Holy Land in what came to be known as the first of nine Crusades. Two centuries later, the crusaders slunk away from Jerusalem for good. The Vatican's primacy degenerated further in 1309, when the newly elected Pope Clement V insisted that the papacy be moved to his native country, France. For the next 68 years, Avignon became the seat of Catholic power. In the waning days of his papacy, Gregory XI returned to Rome in 1377, perhaps due to the persuasions of Catherine of Siena, who would later share the distinction with Francis of Assisi as Italy's only patron saints.

Thereafter all popes would live in Rome, and inside the walls of Vatican City. The Apostolic Palace, architecturally reimagined by Nicholas V in the mid-15th century, would now include the Vatican Library, as well as a secret corridor that would facilitate the popes' safe passage to the Tiber River in the event of an attack. The Renaissance was then dawning, and with it came a number of popes whose patronage of the arts is today vividly on display behind the city walls. Under the watchful eye of Julius II (who was elected despite having had an illegitimate daughter), St. Peter's Basilica was razed in 1506 and then rebuilt to his liking. Later, he cajoled a reluctant Michelangelo into painting the ceiling of the Sistine Chapel. Another distinguished

Renaissance pope, Clement VII, was in fact a member of the Medici family. His eventful papacy includes being held prisoner by an insurgent army for six months, then purchasing his escape, and later commissioning Michelangelo to paint "The Last Judgment."

Though increasingly resplendent with artistic treasures, the Vatican remained wracked with theological discord. The Protestant Reformation of the 1500s begat a Counter-Reformation, metastasizing throughout Europe in the Thirty Years' War. Three hundred years later, in 1868, Pius IX (whose 31 years in the papacy would make him the longest serving elected pope in the Church's history) formed the First Vatican Council. Its purpose was to preserve the doctrine of "papal infallibility," or the belief that popes are blessed with divine revelation and thus immune to error. Being infallible did not make Pius omnipotent, however: Under his reign, the newly formed Republic of Italy reclaimed Vatican land as its final step to unification, prompting the pope to somberly term himself the Prisoner of the Vatican. For the next half century, popes refused to recognize Italy or to leave the walled city.

The standoff came to an end with the Lateran Pacts of 1929, which ratified the Vatican's sovereignty as an internationally recognized territory. The cosignatory of that treaty, Italy's Fascist leader Benito Mussolini, boasted at the time that the arrangement would "bury" the pope's authority, which proved to be a gross misjudgment. But Mussolini did get something out of the treaty: In return, the Vatican agreed to dissolve the Catholic Italian Popular Party, which effectively made Italy a one-party state and ended any pretense of democracy. The Church also

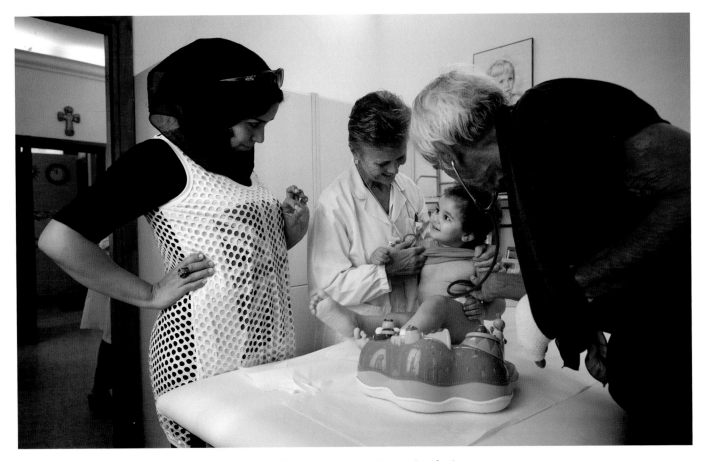

A mother and daughter, originally from Fès, Morocco, receive free medical care at a Vatican clinic for the poor.

received restitution from the government for seized lands; the Vatican invested the money wisely and thereby enjoyed a generous profit from the pacts.

Nonetheless, the other Lateran signatory, Pope Pius XI, opposed fascism and above all Hitler's persecution of Jews. Still, like his successor, Pius XII, who aided the German Resistance during World War II, the pope would be criticized for his conspicuous silence during critical moments in the Third Reich's brutal trajectory. (Regarding such sentiments, Pope Francis would lament to a Spanish newspaper, "Everything which has been thrown at poor Pius XII . . . I do not mean to say that Pius XII did not make mistakes—I make many mistakes myself—but his role must be read in the context of the time.")

The Catholic Church emerged from postwar recriminations due in no small measure to the efforts of Pope John XXIII, who was 76 when the conclave elected him in 1958 after a grueling 11-ballot melodrama. Considering his shaky mandate, John was not expected to do much with his papacy. Nevertheless, in 1962 he called for a Second Vatican Council that in subtle but unmistakable ways brought the Church into the 20th century. Ornateness would be downplayed, Latin deemphasized; no reaffirmation of rigorous dogma would be issued. John XXIII died of cancer in 1963, less than five years into his papacy. But a half century later, Pope Francis would declare him *"il buon Papa,"* the Good Pope, and he would be canonized along with the man who had succeeded him 15 years later: John Paul II.

John Paul's 27-year papacy (the second longest of elected popes after that of Pius IX) was a double-edged sword for the Church. On the one hand, the charismatic, upbeat Pole restored the papacy's international standing. His indefatigable opposition to communism (in particular, the spiritual inspiration he lent to his Polish countrymen in their resistance to the Soviet Union) is widely held to have been key in the collapse of that movement. A steadfast conservative, John Paul nonetheless expressed tolerance for gays, acceptance of evolution, and deep opposition to capital punishment and apartheid—and in so doing he presented a more welcoming face of Catholicism. In 1981, the pope had arrived at St. Peter's Square for a public audience when a gunman belonging to a Turkish fascist group shot him several times before being wrestled to the ground. John Paul lost three-fourths of his blood but miraculously survived. Two years later, he met with his would-be assassin in prison and pardoned him.

At the same time, the Church's laxity toward sex abuse in the clergy tainted John Paul II's papacy. "His experience in Poland had been that the secret police would accuse priests of this sort of thing all the time, so he just didn't believe it," says Father Thomas Reese of the *National Catholic Reporter*. It was not until 2002, after the *Boston Globe* published a series of investigative stories on abuse cases, that the pope addressed a meeting of American cardinals on the matter. But by that time scandal after scandal had indelibly scarred the Catholic Church's reputation. That scar was far from healed by the time of John Paul's death in 2005.

Combined with emerging financial scandals and the so-called Vatileaks episode of 2012—in which Pope Benedict's butler leaked numerous internal documents to the press alleging corruption and blackmail—an uneasy consensus was beginning to form from numerous bishops and cardinals around the world.

In their belief, the traditions of the Vatican were in need of drastic reappraisal. And so came Pope Francis.

CEREMONIES
and
CELEBRATIONS

Ivory robes, glistening relics, time-honored recitations—the spirit of the Vatican and its ceremonies are deeply and uniquely intertwined. Royals and bishops attend open-air Masses alongside throngs of pilgrims who camp out to reserve a spot within view. Indoor ceremonies, if quieter, carry the same weight: a constancy that has steadied the Church through the twists and turns of the times.

Previous pages: In its timeless majesty, St. Peter's Basilica is sacred ground for the world's 1.2 billion Roman Catholics.

Below: The Holy Father in his liturgical vestments celebrates Mass on Vatican grounds.

Opposite: He also celebrates Mass in other locations, such as an All Saints' Day Mass in Verano Cemetery, Rome.

The pope doesn't wield armies.
He can't impose sanctions.
But he can speak with
great moral authority, and
it makes a difference.

I would not speak about "absolute" truths, even for believers . . . Truth is a relationship. As such, each one of us receives the truth and expresses it from within, that is to say, according to one's own circumstances, culture, and situation in life.

POPE FRANCIS

From my point of view, God is the light that illuminates the darkness, even if it does not dissolve it, and a spark of divine light is within each of us.

POPE FRANCIS

The branches of the Christmas tree in St. Peter's Square frame Pope Francis on the steps of the basilica.

Pages 168–169: With the Nativity scene behind him, the pontiff speaks with children during a Christmas Eve Mass.

Opposite: Holding a monstrance, Pope Francis leads the New Year's Eve vespers.

Below: The pope leads a Mass for the Corpus Domini, 60 days after Easter

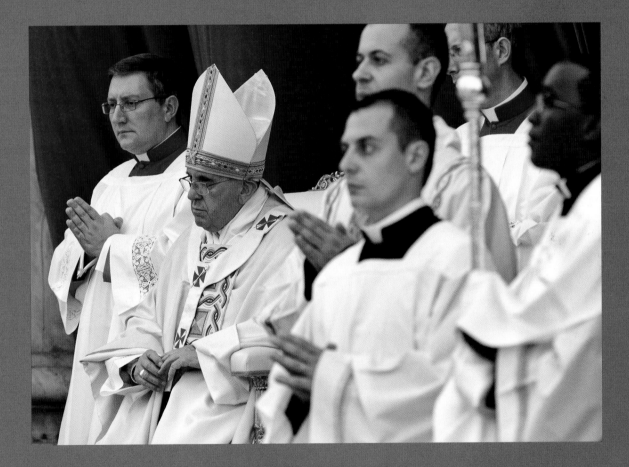

Pope Francis presides over a Eucharistic celebration at a Mass to mark the Feast of Our Lady of Guadalupe, the patron saint of Mexico.

Previous pages: A bird's-eye view from above St. Peter's high altar highlights the grandeur of the basilica.

Cardinals (in red) and bishops (in purple) line up to meet Pope Francis toward the end of one of Wednesday's general audiences.

Let us never lose hope!
God loves us always, even with
our mistakes and sins.

POPE FRANCIS

To be saints is not a privilege for the few, but a vocation for everyone.

POPE FRANCIS

The Sistine Chapel Choir performs during a Christmas Eve Mass.

Following pages: After delivering his Christmas address to the Roman Curia (the administrative body that assists the pope in the exercise of his office), Pope Francis greets members in the Sala Clementina in the Apostolic Palace.

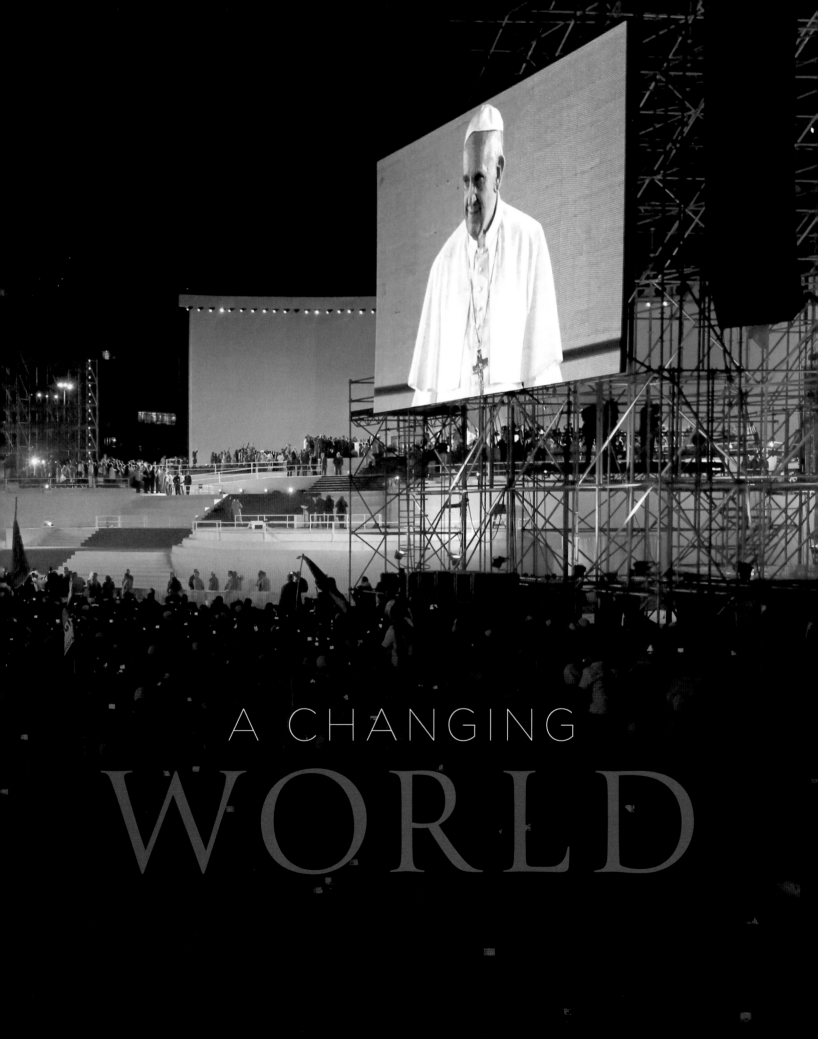

A CHANGING
WORLD

Pages 190–191: The Vatican uses the latest technology to give Pope Francis broad access to the faithful. Here he speaks from giant screens to young people gathered on Copacabana beach in Rio de Janeiro, Brazil, for the 28th World Youth Day.

Throngs of pilgrims attending World Youth Day in July 2013 spent the night sleeping on Copacabana beach in Rio de Janeiro, Brazil, before attending the final Mass.

On the morning of Sunday, April 27, 2014, some 800,000 pilgrims from all over the world poured into Rome and across the Tiber River into Vatican City to witness the canonization of Popes John Paul II and John XXIII. Even for jaded lifers of the Eternal City, the spectacle along St. Peter's Square was astounding: innumerable young travelers stretched out on sleeping bags as if for a rock festival; guitar-strumming priests and nuns hunched under umbrellas to ward off the sunlight; papal banners and signs of the images of the soon-to-be-canonized popes flying overhead. Immense closed-circuit screens were set up throughout Rome to accommodate the thousands who could not squeeze themselves into the piazza. Together in worshipful silence they listened to Pope Francis's stirring tribute to his two papal predecessors: "They were priests, and bishops and popes of the 20th century. They lived through the

. . . time seems to stand still in the moments when Francis encounters the afflicted.

tragic events of that century, but they were not overwhelmed by them. For them, God was more powerful; faith was more powerful—faith in Jesus Christ the Redeemer of man and the Lord of history; the mercy of God, shown by those five wounds, was more powerful; and more powerful too was the closeness of Mary our Mother."

For the uninitiated viewer tuning in to cable television that day, the solemnity and momentousness of the canonization served as an arresting testimonial: Even today, in a world of multicultural enmeshment and ongoing visual bombardment, the papal execution of ancient Catholic rites remains an object of abiding fascination. Or, to put it simply: The pope—especially this pope—knows how to draw a crowd.

CLOSING THE DISTANCE

During 2014, the first full year of Francis's papacy, some 5.9 million visitors came to the Vatican—almost triple the number who visited in 2012, during his predecessor Benedict's final year. More than half of these visitors attended the Angelus prayer that the pope conducts from an open window of the Apostolic Palace every Sunday at noon. Another 1.2 million showed up at one of the 43 general audiences held on Wednesday mornings on the steps of the basilica—a stupefying average of 27,900 pilgrims standing outside on the hard stone of St. Peter's Square for each event, at times for hours under Rome's withering heat. All of this for the opportunity to witness (and photograph), free of charge, the man that author Massimo Franco refers to as a "contradiction in terms": the Available Pope.

Two new features of the Wednesday Mass accompany Francis's papacy. The first is the open-topped vehicle that ferries him through the crowd, known as the Popemobile—a motorized version of the *sedia gestatoria* (ceremonial seat) upon which popes were hoisted and carried around all the way through the short-lived papacy of John Paul I in 1978. The white, jeeplike Fiat Campagnola conveying John Paul II was fitted on all sides with bulletproof glass following the assassination attempt on him in 1981.

After spending the first year's worth of Wednesdays behind glass, Pope Francis judged the experience to be antiseptic, akin to a "sardine can," and symbolically discordant with his belief that the Church step out from behind the walls and extend itself to the world's periphery. He ordered the glass removed, later saying: "It's true that anything could happen, but let's face it, at my age I don't have much to lose." (Though not for public display, it happens that Pope Francis also has a Popemobile of his own for whenever he wishes to get behind the wheel in Vatican City: a white 1984 Renault economy car an Italian priest gave him with 186,000 miles already on it.)

In the minutes before his Wednesday morning homilies, the pope's custom is to trundle slowly through the exultant throngs at St. Peter's Square in the glass-free version of the white Mercedes, standing from the backseat papal throne and waving. Pilgrims cry out and fling flowers and T-shirts, which the security team trotting valiantly alongside attempts (with varying success) to intercept before they land against the pope. Often he instructs his driver to stop so he can mingle with the crowd. More than once at his behest the

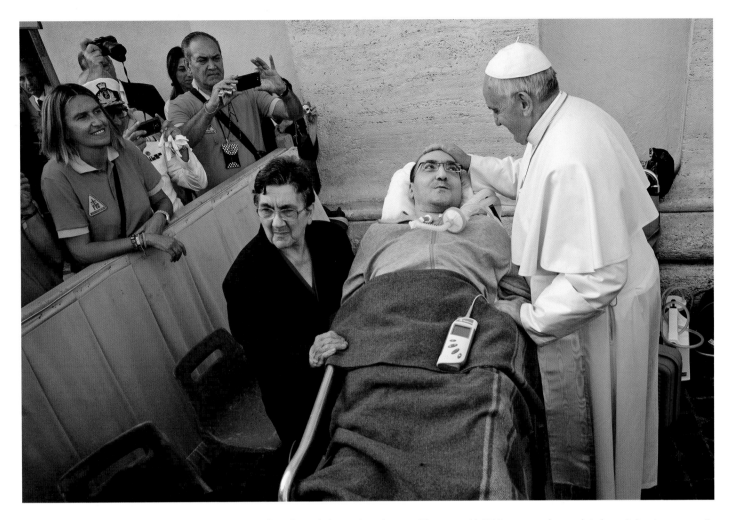

Pope Francis blesses Salvatore D'argento, who is paralyzed from the neck down. About the pope D'argento said, "He's a person that needs to be met. A unique person."

Popemobile has taken random and plainly delighted bystanders for a spin around the square.

One attendee who was awarded an impromptu ride on a Wednesday morning in October 2013 was an Italian teenager with Down syndrome. That widely televised gesture marks the second change in Wednesday general audiences under Francis—a change of subtle but even greater symbolic value than the removal of the bulletproof glass. The pope has made it a point to bring the physically disabled—"the least of these," those bearing "the glorious wounds of Christ"—to the center of the Church's view. It is not simply that dozens of physically challenged visitors in

their wheelchairs are positioned near the foot of the steps from which the pope gives his homilies, as has been the custom in previous papacies. It is how time seems to stand still in the moments when Francis encounters the afflicted.

Among the classic images of this pope is that of him stopping on St. Peter's Square to embrace and pray with a man whose face was covered in tumors. That moment of fraternal benevolence was echoed seven months later outside Vatican City, when Francis was traveling by car through Calabria in southern Italy. Spotting a sign on the roadside asking him to pull over "to see an angel who has been waiting for you," the pope did so. He found a young

woman named Roberta, confined to her bed since birth and unable to breath without machine assistance. Francis kissed her and prayed for her while a small crowd of Roberta's friends and family exclaimed, *"Bravo, Papa Francesco! Grazie! Grazie!"*

As one of them later wrote on Facebook, "Here are gestures in life that are worth more than speeches . . ."

THE PILGRIMAGE REVIVED

The pilgrims come to the Vatican in numbers great and small, with varying degrees of fanfare. Among them was a delegation of blind Italians. Francis encouraged them to "greet each other with our limits." Another audience he received was the Little Mission for the Deaf and Mute,

with whom he discussed the "culture of encounter" as it applies to the marginalized. Many visitors are Catholic youths. In August 2013, a group of grinning teenagers from an Italian diocese cajoled the pope into taking what would be the first papal "selfie" with them; it became an overnight media sensation. Other pilgrims join their Catholic religious leaders on the voyage to Rome, such as the group accompanying the archbishop of the war-ravaged Central African Republic. The pope singled them out after Mass, saying that he wished to "encourage the Central African people, who are harshly tried, to walk with faith and hope."

Countless choirs from Catholic churches and schools all over the world have scrounged up money to perform before the pope at Vatican services—

President Barack Obama has described himself as a "great admirer" of the pontiff.

including choral groups from Macon, Georgia; West Toledo, Ohio; and Erlanger, Kentucky. Charity and ecumenical groups have likewise pinched pennies to make the journey.

More elaborately, more than 2,000 knights and ladies of the Equestrian Order of the Holy Sepulchre of Jerusalem—established at the time of the First Crusade as an occupying troop during the brief conquest of Jerusalem—convened in the Vatican's Paul VI Audience Hall in September 2013. Members traveled from all over the world to receive their ritual once-every-five-years blessing from their spiritual leader. A far more irregular pilgrimage took place in August 2014, when the Buenos Aires–based San Lorenzo soccer team—the pope's favorite since childhood—arrived in Rome to present their fellow Argentine with the Copa Libertadores trophy, the prize of the most prestigious championship in Latin America. Though it was the first time the club had won in its 107-year history, Francis insisted that the achievement be kept in perspective: "I am very happy about it, but no, it is not a miracle."

In March 2014, Pope Francis welcomed a pilgrim from across the Atlantic Ocean who described himself as a "great admirer": Barack Obama. The first African-American president joined the first Latin American pope in the Papal Library and presented him with a chest filled with fruit and vegetable seeds used in the White House garden. The chest was made of wood reclaimed from the Basilica of the National Shrine of the Assumption of the Blessed Virgin Mary in Baltimore, Maryland. In return, the pope presented the president with two symbolic medallions, in addition to a leather-bound edition of *The Joy of the Gospel*. "I actually will probably read this when I'm in the Oval Office, when I am deeply frustrated—and I am sure it will give me strength," said President Obama.

After their 52-minute meeting, Pope Francis continued with his daily schedule. He had other pilgrims to receive, including several bishops from the deeply impoverished country of Madagascar, whom he urged to "call out without fear to all Malagasy society, and especially its leaders, with regard to the issue of poverty, which is largely due to corruption and lack of attention to the common good."

Some of the pilgrims do not come from far at all, but their message carries louder than the proclamation of a foreign dignitary. One day during the fall of 2014, the head of the Vatican's Office of Papal Charities, or almoner, Cardinal Konrad Krajewski, encountered a homeless man from Sardinia. He met Franco on Via della Conciliazione, the wide boulevard that dead-ends into St. Peter's Square. As it was Franco's 50th birthday, the cardinal offered to buy him dinner. Franco took some persuading. He reeked, he informed the almoner, showers being harder to come by in Rome than food. When Krajewski reported this conversation to Pope Francis, an idea was hatched. A month later, three shower stalls were installed in the public restrooms of St. Peter's Square.

BEYOND ROME

The notion of a pope out in the world, beyond the walls of Vatican City, was until fairly recently a dubious one. Geographic and physical challenges of the times, political instability, and ever shifting intrigues within the Church made travel even within Rome seem imprudent. Martin I's four-year papacy was cut short in 653, when he was arrested beyond the walls of Vatican City, apparently while inside the Lateran Palace. He would then be dragged to Constantinople and ultimately exiled to the Crimea. During the eighth century, Pope Stephen II ventured abroad by crossing the Alps to crown his ally, the Frankish king Pippin the Younger (the father of Charlemagne). Pope Urban II (1088–1099) was notably intrepid, having voyaged to France to rally

Pope Francis has sent reverberations through-out the world of international diplomacy . . .

Christians into mounting a recapture of the Holy Land, in what would become the First Crusade. And in 1804, Pius VII arrived in Paris to crown Napoleon in hopes of gaining concessions from the ruler, who instead later arrested Pius and exiled him to Savona (though in 1814 the pope would return to Rome, while Napoleon was defeated and banished to Elba).

But papal travel outside Europe did not exist until 1964, when Paul VI—the soon-to-be-named "Pilgrim Pope"—arrived in the Holy Land, becoming the first pope ever to sojourn by airplane. Paul later visited Portugal and Africa and was undeterred when, at the Manila airport in 1970, a man stabbed him with a knife: The would-be assassin was apprehended, the 73-year-old pope was suitably mended, and thereafter he proceeded with the day's schedule.

Yet Paul VI was an agoraphobe compared with John Paul II. During his 27-year papacy, John Paul revolutionized the pope's persona in the international arena. In all, he made 104 foreign trips, often to places to which a pastoral visit had hitherto been unthinkable: Papua New Guinea, Azerbaijan, Iceland, the Solomon Islands, and Rwanda, in addition to 124 other countries. John Paul II's most stirring international voyage was in 1979, when he returned home to Poland (after Paul VI had twice been refused entry there) and declared before three million of his countrymen in Warsaw's Victory Square, as a stinging rebuke to the Communist government, "It is impossible without Christ to understand this nation."

Pope Francis has sent reverberations throughout the world of international diplomacy in ways that seem certain to eclipse John Paul II's influence. Some of this owes to Francis's sheer popularity. A Pew Research worldwide poll conducted in December 2014 found that a whopping 84 percent of Europeans, including non-Catholics, rated him favorably, as did 78 percent of Americans—numbers that no national politician in any of those countries approaches. (Even in the Muslim-dominant Middle East, where the pope rated most negatively, as many respondents viewed him positively as unfavorably.) In 2014, *Fortune* ranked him the world's greatest leader. That distinction would most likely get no argument from the long list of state executives who have paid homage to Francis at the Vatican—Angela Merkel, Vladimir Putin, and François Hollande among them, in addition to Obama and Argentina's President Kirchner.

Francis has not shied from using the political capital garnered from his popularity to interpose himself in diplomatic episodes. His presence was especially prominent during his 2014 trip to the Middle East, when he persuaded Israel's President Shimon Peres and Palestine's President Mahmoud Abbas to travel to the Vatican and join him in "an intense prayer session" with the aim of providing a peace settlement. Earlier, the pope conducted a prayer vigil as the Obama Administration was contemplating air strikes on Syria; following his efforts, the U.S. government agreed to abandon any plans for military aggression. And, as officials from both the United States and Cuba would later acknowledge, the pope played a crucial behind-the-scenes role in reopening diplomatic relations between the two countries—including hosting secret meetings at the Vatican where the delegations hammered out the final agreement.

Pope Francis prays in front of the Western Wall in Jerusalem's Old City as Rabbi Shmuel Rabinowitz, Rabbi of the Western Wall and the Holy Sites, watches.

If, owing to his age, Pope Francis is unlikely to surpass John Paul II's 721,052 miles of travel, it is nonetheless clear that he will encounter masses unprecedented in the annals of Catholicism. That was certainly the case in July 2013, during his first overseas trip to Brazil in his native continent. At a youth event on Copacabana Beach in Rio de Janeiro, an estimated 3.7 million cheered on the pope as he declared from a stage, "The Church needs you, your enthusiasm, your creativity, and the joy that is so characteristic of you!"

But his more pointed homilies have often been directed to smaller groups, such as the South American bishops he met with on that same trip, in Rio's Cathedral of San Sebastian. The address he delivered to them was long and entirely of his authorship, word for word. Promoting "the culture of encounter," Francis urged them to have "the courage to go against the tide of this culture of efficiency" and to instead "find ways to spend time with" the young—emphasizing that the encounter must begin "on the outskirts, with those who are farthest away, with those who do not usually go to church. They are the VIPs who are invited. Go and search for them at the crossroads."

Similarly, Francis carried a decidedly sharp message to the bishops of Korea in August 2014. Declaring in effect that all politics is local, he instructed them to be accountable to their parish priests: "Where I come from, some priests would tell me, 'I've called the bishop, I've asked to meet him; yet three months have gone by, and I have still not received an answer.' Brothers, if a priest phones today and asks to see you, call him back immediately, today or tomorrow."

Pages 202–203: Hands stretch out for Pope Francis, who greets the crowd of faithful from his Popemobile in downtown Rio de Janeiro during the summer of 2013 on his first foreign trip as pontiff.

People respond to the pope during a general audience, and his simplicity and humility seem to electrify the crowd.

MESSAGE OF MERCY

Invariably Francis uses his pilgrimages to throw light on the twin themes of his papacy: The Catholic Church should be "for the poor," and it should actively seek them out. Nowhere was that mission made more evident than on his first trip, on July 8, 2013, a little over three months after his election. His destination was Lampedusa, a small Sicilian island that has become home to thousands of North African refugees, many of them Muslims fleeing the chaos in Libya and now seeking asylum in Italy. They arrived by sea after a treacherous voyage that some had not survived. Upon arrival, the Pope met with several of the refugees. One told Francis that he made it to Lampedusa only after paying a human trafficker a large sum of money. The pope mentioned this in his homily later that day: "I recently heard one of these brothers. Before arriving here, he had passed through the hands of traffickers—those who exploit the poverty of others; these people for whom the poverty of others is a source of income."

While saluting the local community for showing compassion to the migrants, Francis challenged the world to resist "the globalization of indifference" toward the needy. And, in what would soon become another distinct trait of his papacy, Francis also paid tribute to the refugees' faith: "I give a thought, too, to the dear Muslim immigrants that are beginning the fast of Ramadan, with best wishes for abundant spiritual fruits. The Church is near to you in the search for a more dignified life for yourselves and for your families." He then added a greeting in the Lampedusan dialect: "I say to you, *O' schia!*"

His travel has been notable for its bias toward the neglected. Whereas Pope Benedict's first three trips abroad were to the European nations of Germany, Poland, and Spain, Francis selected Brazil for his maiden voyage. On the plane back to Rome, he described the Brazilians to the traveling press as inspiring in the face of their poverty: "They are a very lovable people, a people who like to celebrate, who even amid suffering always find a path to seek out the good somewhere." The spectacle of all those young people on Copacabana Beach was, he said, stunning. If anything, he regretted not being able to mingle with them more.

The new Pope then shared a striking lament. "With less security," he told the *Vaticanisti*, "I could have been with the people, I could have embraced them, greeted them, without armored cars . . . There is security in trusting a people. It is true that there is always the danger of some mad person—the danger that some mad person will do something. But then there is the Lord! But to make an armed space between the bishop and the people is madness, and I prefer the other madness: Away with it! And run the risk of the other madness! I prefer this madness: Away with it! Closeness is good for us all."

Not until his fourth trip would he visit a Western European nation—in that case, France. By that point, he had already traveled to the Middle East, South Korea, and Albania. The latter he chose as his first European destination outside Italy because, he said, the country had demonstrated its commitment to religious harmony by electing a government in which Christians and Muslims shared power. Francis arrived there in September 2014, on the heels of death threats publicly made against him by the Islamic extremist group ISIS. In defiance of the threats (and evidently at the pope's behest), Vatican officials informed the press that they did not intend to take extra security precautions, and that Francis planned to tour the Albanian crowd in his open-topped Popemobile. His homily in Tirana minced

no words on the subject of ISIS: Such groups, he said, "perverted" religion. He added, "To kill in the name of God is a grave sacrilege. To discriminate in the name of God is inhuman."

In January 2015, Francis traveled to Asia for the first time. In the island country of Sri Lanka—where 40 costumed elephants were among those to greet him at the airport—he undertook many of the symbolic gestures that have become emblematic of his trips. He paid tribute to the Christian believers in the Buddhist-majority nation by canonizing Sri Lanka's first saint, a 17th-century missionary named Joseph Vaz. He visited the war-torn north of the country, where decades of civil strife ended in 2009 with the Sinhalese Buddhist government's brutal defeat of the Tamil Hindus. He met with religious leaders from the Buddhist, Hindu, and Muslim communities to urge reconciliation. In a speech before an open-air mass audience, he called on the newly elected Sri Lankan government to account for war crimes.

And there was a new flourish to this trip: Pope Francis gave all his speeches in English for the first time. Perhaps it was a rehearsal for his travel in September 2015 to the United States, a country he had never visited previously.

ACTIONS THAT SPEAK LOUDLY

Some of the pope's travels are with a single precise purpose in mind. In July 2014, he flew by helicopter 130 miles south of Rome to Caserta to meet with a local pastor named Giovanni Traettino and speak at his church. It was the first time that a pope had ever visited an Evangelical church. Months earlier at Santa Marta, Francis had met with Argentine friends from the Evangelical community. They requested that he offer a gesture of support to the many Italians of that faith who suffered persecution during the Fascist era.

By that point, he had already traveled to the Middle East, South Korea, and Albania.

The friends mentioned Pastor Traettino and reminded Francis that they had met in 2006, when then Archbishop Bergoglio famously asked 7,000 Evangelicals and Catholics to pray for him at Luna Park. As an echo of that ecumenical outreach, the pope informed his staff that he wished to go to Caserta. Once at the Evangelical Church of Reconciliation, he publicly acknowledged Catholic complicity in the Fascist persecutions, adding: "I ask for your forgiveness for those Catholic brothers and sisters who didn't know and were tempted by the devil."

These remarks were made on the Pope's second trip to Caserta in as many days. Word of his planned visit to the church had caused consternation among the Catholic townsfolk, who felt overlooked. Francis mollified them by flying in one day before his Evangelical encounter to address the local celebrants during their annual Feast of St. Anne. But even that event—an open-air Mass attended by some 200,000—conveyed a succinct message: It was an attack on the local Camorra Mafia, whose illegal toxic-waste dumping had bespoiled the regional landscape and diseased the

The pope greets a visitor to the Vatican. Prince and Grand Master of the Order of Malta Fra' Matthew Festing stands at the pope's right.

populace. (A month earlier in the Mafia stronghold of Calabria, Francis had issued especially blistering words on the subject: The Calabrian 'Ndrangheta, Francis said, promote "adoration of evil and contempt of the common good" and were therefore "excommunicated.")

Francis plots even his ceremonial trips with great care for the symbolic weight they will inevitably carry. For example, several European cities requested that the pope visit them to mark the occasion of World War I's centennial in September 2014. He chose Redipuglia, in northeastern Italy, where the country's largest sacrarium contains the remains of more than 100,000 Italian soldiers. But just before visiting the famed mausoleum, Francis stopped to walk in the nearby, largely overlooked Austro-Hungarian cemetery, where nearly 15,000 soldiers who fought against Italy are buried. With his silent solemn stroll, the pope conveyed a poignant message—one that he would underscore minutes later in his homily at the Italian memorial: "War is madness . . . From this place we remember all the victims of every war."

In his Redipuglia speech, the Pope invoked the word "brother" several times, as he nearly always does. For all of the revolutionary fervor attributed to Francis, the messages he delivers are simple and distinctly old-fashioned. The cell phone–less, computer-less leader of the Catholic Church frequently decries 21st-century self-absorption, the breakneck frenzy of humanity, and the overall aversion to the fundamentals of "the encounter." Yet to be a street-wise *porteño* is also to recognize the world as it is. And so in September of 2014 Pope Francis gave an unflinching nod to the information age. He held what could be termed the first ever papal digital pilgrimage, an online Google Hangout with students from five continents. When one of them asked him about the future, the pope displayed his characteristic balance between traditionalism and idealism: "If you have wings and roots, you own the future," he told the students. "You need the wings to fly, dream, and believe. But you need roots to receive the wisdom from the elderly."

REACHING FULL CIRCLE

With gentle forcefulness—in Vatican City, throughout the world, and now through cyberspace—Pope Francis spreads the message of a new Church that in fact harks back to its beginnings. His most radical utterances—such as "Who am I to judge?"—are inextricably basic to Christianity, and indeed to the tenets of any civil society. With the timelessness of his plainspoken wisdom, he has paradoxically achieved preeminence on the global stage. As *Time*'s Nancy Gibbs put it when the magazine named Francis Person of the Year in 2014: "He has placed himself at the very center of the central conversations of our time: about wealth and poverty, fairness and justice, transparency, modernity, globalization, the role of women, the nature of marriage, the temptations of power."

Exactly how he will influence those conversations, and ultimately how history will view Pope Francis, is too early to say. The only certainty is that he will exceed the typically modest goal he set for himself when replying to a reporter's question on the subject: "I have not thought about this. But I like it when you recall someone and say 'He was a good guy, he did what he could, and he was not that bad.' With that, I would be content."

The
POPE
of the
PEOPLE

Championing the Church as a home for everybody, Pope Francis has captivated the world with his message of mercy. Visitors journey across continents to experience that ineffable charisma that characterizes his presence, his words, his touch. Washing the feet of young prisoners, embracing the suffering—the pope lifts the people in the same way he is reenergizing the 2,000-year-old institution to which they flock.

Pages 212–213: From humble beginnings as a
callejero, or street priest, to worldwide acclaim as
Holy Father, the pope has delighted those around him.

Previous pages: Tens of thousands of people attend
the Wednesday general audiences in St. Peter's Square,
waiting for hours to get a glimpse of the pope.

Above: Pope Francis is known for his infectious laugh.

Below: A young girl at the parish of St. Joseph all'Aurelio in Rome reacts with joy to the arrival of Pope Francis during a papal visit.

A party atmosphere settles on St. Peter's Square as pilgrims arrive for the 2014 Canonization Mass of Pope John Paul II and Pope John XXIII.

I see clearly that the thing the church needs most today is the ability to heal wounds and to warm the hearts of the faithful; it needs nearness, proximity. I see the church as a field hospital after battle.

POPE FRANCIS

Some 800,000 pilgrims came to Rome to witness the April 2014 canonization of Pope John Paul II and Pope John XXIII.

Previous pages: Some visitors to the Vatican use the opportunity for cheering and exultation.

A nun and others like her also use the opportunity as a time for reflection.

Above: To get as close as possible, a man holds a
young boy over a barricade during a general audience.

The gift of piety means to be truly capable of rejoicing with those who rejoice, of weeping with those who weep, of being close to those who are lonely or in anguish, of correcting those in error, of consoling the afflicted, of welcoming and helping those in need.

POPE FRANCIS

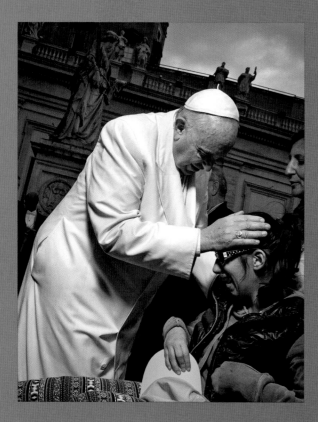

Previous pages: With cameras ready and arms raised, the crowd at a general audience shares both a physical and a spiritual closeness.

Above: The Holy Father blesses a visitor in a wheelchair. The pope has remarked that God offers "an accompanying presence, a history of goodness which touches every story of suffering and opens up a ray of light."

A young girl, along with other faithful, waits for the pope during a general audience.

This is important: to get to know people, listen, expand the circle of ideas. The world is crisscrossed by roads that come closer together and move apart, but the important thing is that they lead towards the Good.

POPE FRANCIS

Previous pages: People of all ages gather at the barricades in hopes of touching the beloved pope.

Above: The pope lives up to his remark: "An evangelizer must never look like someone who has just come back from a funeral."

Below: With technology at everyone's fingertips, the pope's words and pictures are readily disseminated.

Following pages: The power of faith brims over for parishioners in St. Peter's Square as Pope Francis extends his touch.

THE PAPAL LEGACY

The papal lineage begins with St. Peter, the disciple the Gospels say Jesus Christ chose to be the symbolic "rock" on which his Church would be built. St. Peter was the first in an unbroken succession of leaders who by the fourth century were known as popes and played pivotal roles in the power struggles of Europe.

"St. Peter," by
Peter Paul Rubens

BISHOPS OF ROME
Little is known about the first leaders of the Church, who would come to be known as the bishops of Rome, a title still held by popes today. The earliest popes are all considered saints by the Catholic Church.

St. Clement I
Said to have been tied to an anchor, thrown in the Black Sea

0
A.D.

10

Jesus Christ crucified

ST. GREGORY THE GREAT
The first monk to be elected pope, he consolidates papal territories and helps shift the Church's focus from the fading Roman Empire toward Western Europe, initiating the conversion of the British Isles to Christianity.

"St. Gregory the Great," by Francisco de Goya

SAECULUM OBSCURUM
From 872 to 1012, the papacy falls under a dark period of corruption. In the Cadaver Synod of 897, Pope Stephen VII has the corpse of his predecessor disinterred, garbed in papal robes, and put on trial.

"Pope Formosus and Stephen VII," by Jean-Paul Laurens

St. Gregory III
Last pope from Asia (Syria)

500   600   700   800   900

Forces led by Muhammad conquer Mecca, ushering in the age of Islam

Umayyads conquer the Iberian Peninsula

The Frankish king Pépin establishes the first papal states with a donation of territory

Pépin's son Charlemagne is crowned Holy Roman Emperor by Pope Saint Leo III

Arabs raid Rome, sacking Old St. Peter's

John VIII First pope to be assassinated

THE AVIGNON PAPACY
With political instability in Italy, Clement V moves the papacy to Avignon, France, marking a period of French influence, and works to divert the warriors of feuding European countries into the Crusades.

THE WESTERN SCHISM
A split within the Catholic Church from 1378 to 1417 sees three rival popes vying for authority. The election of Martin V by cardinals from all three factions secures the line of Roman popes as legitimate.

Alexander VI of the Borgia family has multiple mistresses and illegitimate children. His son, Cesare, becomes a cardinal and the model for Machiavelli's *The Prince*.

RENAISSANCE RULERS
Powerful Italian families dominate the papacy during the Renaissance period. Their reigns are known for decadence and nepotism but also for a flourishing of the arts under their generous patronage.

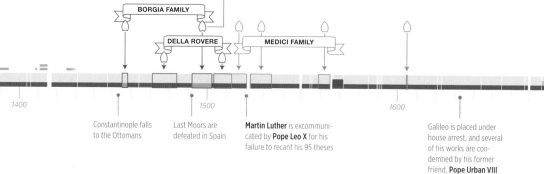

BORGIA FAMILY

DELLA ROVERE   MEDICI FAMILY

Gregory XI
Moves the papacy back to Rome; last French pope

1300   1400   1500   1600   1700

Constantinople falls to the Ottomans

Last Moors are defeated in Spain

Martin Luther is excommunicated by **Pope Leo X** for his failure to recant his 95 theses

Galileo is placed under house arrest, and several of his works are condemned by his former friend, **Pope Urban VIII**

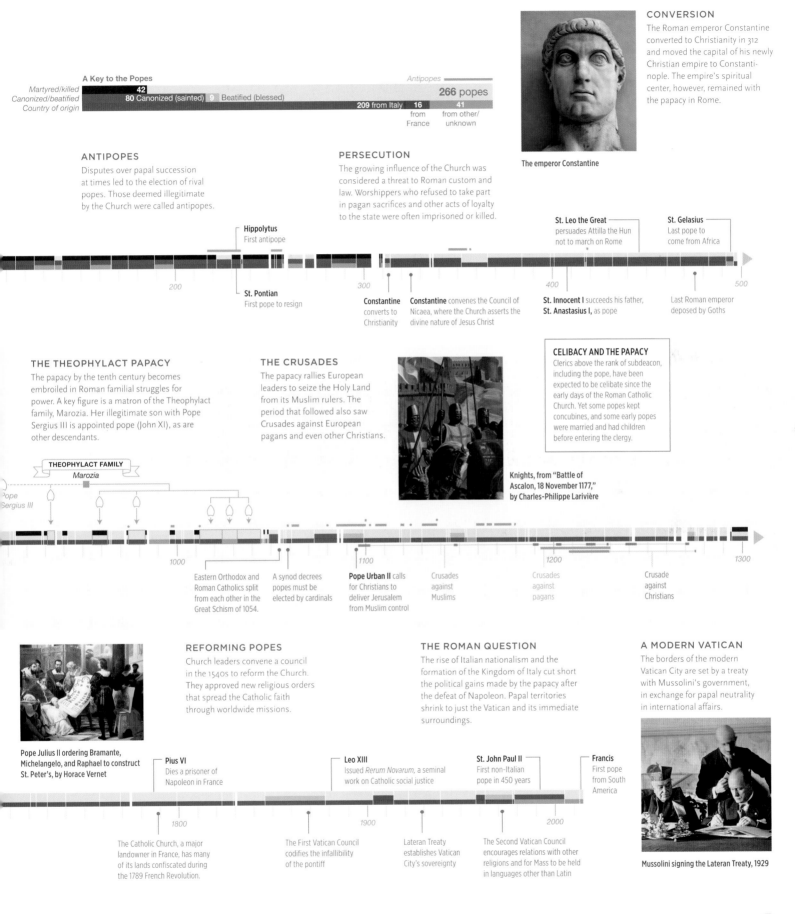

CONVERSION

The Roman emperor Constantine converted to Christianity in 312 and moved the capital of his newly Christian empire to Constantinople. The empire's spiritual center, however, remained with the papacy in Rome.

The emperor Constantine

A Key to the Popes

Martyred/killed	**42**		*Antipopes*
Canonized/beatified	**80** Canonized (sainted) **9** Beatified (blessed)		**266** popes
Country of origin		**209** from Italy **16** **41**	
		from France	from other/ unknown

ANTIPOPES

Disputes over papal succession at times led to the election of rival popes. Those deemed illegitimate by the Church were called antipopes.

PERSECUTION

The growing influence of the Church was considered a threat to Roman custom and law. Worshippers who refused to take part in pagan sacrifices and other acts of loyalty to the state were often imprisoned or killed.

Hippolytus
First antipope

St. Leo the Great
persuades Attilla the Hun not to march on Rome

St. Gelasius
Last pope to come from Africa

200 *300* *400* *500*

St. Pontian
First pope to resign

Constantine
converts to Christianity

Constantine convenes the Council of Nicaea, where the Church asserts the divine nature of Jesus Christ

St. Innocent I succeeds his father, **St. Anastasius I,** as pope

Last Roman emperor deposed by Goths

THE THEOPHYLACT PAPACY

The papacy by the tenth century becomes embroiled in Roman familial struggles for power. A key figure is a matron of the Theophylact family, Marozia. Her illegitimate son with Pope Sergius III is appointed pope (John XI), as are other descendants.

THE CRUSADES

The papacy rallies European leaders to seize the Holy Land from its Muslim rulers. The period that followed also saw Crusades against European pagans and even other Christians.

CELIBACY AND THE PAPACY

Clerics above the rank of subdeacon, including the pope, have been expected to be celibate since the early days of the Roman Catholic Church. Yet some popes kept concubines, and some early popes were married and had children before entering the clergy.

Knights, from "Battle of Ascalon, 18 November 1177," by Charles-Philippe Larivière

THEOPHYLACT FAMILY
Marozia

Pope Sergius III

1000 *1100* *1200* *1300*

Eastern Orthodox and Roman Catholics split from each other in the Great Schism of 1054.

A synod decrees popes must be elected by cardinals

Pope Urban II calls for Christians to deliver Jerusalem from Muslim control

Crusades against Muslims

Crusades against pagans

Crusade against Christians

REFORMING POPES

Church leaders convene a council in the 1540s to reform the Church. They approved new religious orders that spread the Catholic faith through worldwide missions.

THE ROMAN QUESTION

The rise of Italian nationalism and the formation of the Kingdom of Italy cut short the political gains made by the papacy after the defeat of Napoleon. Papal territories shrink to just the Vatican and its immediate surroundings.

A MODERN VATICAN

The borders of the modern Vatican City are set by a treaty with Mussolini's government, in exchange for papal neutrality in international affairs.

Pope Julius II ordering Bramante, Michelangelo, and Raphael to construct St. Peter's, by Horace Vernet

Pius VI
Dies a prisoner of Napoleon in France

Leo XIII
Issued *Rerum Novarum*, a seminal work on Catholic social justice

St. John Paul II
First non-Italian pope in 450 years

Francis
First pope from South America

1800 *1900* *2000*

The Catholic Church, a major landowner in France, has many of its lands confiscated during the 1789 French Revolution.

The First Vatican Council codifies the infallibility of the pontiff

Lateran Treaty establishes Vatican City's sovereignty

The Second Vatican Council encourages relations with other religions and for Mass to be held in languages other than Latin

Mussolini signing the Lateran Treaty, 1929

CATHOLIC SHIFT

From 1900 to 2015, the number of Catholics worldwide more than quadrupled from an estimated 266.6 million to more than 1.2 billion. As a percentage of the global population, the number of Catholics has remained steady at just under 17 percent throughout that time period.

While growing consistently, the Catholic population has shifted geographically. In 1900, more than two-thirds of the world's Catholics lived in Europe; as of 2015, fewer than a quarter do. In the century between 1910 and 2010, the percentage of Catholics worldwide who lived in Latin America and the Caribbean, North America, Sub-Saharan Africa, and Asia and the Pacific grew by approximately 15 percentage points, 3 percentage points, 15 percentage points, and 7 percentage points respectively. The United States' Catholic population grew from roughly 10.7 million people to 74.7 million.

The maps that follow show percentages of the world's Catholic population by country.

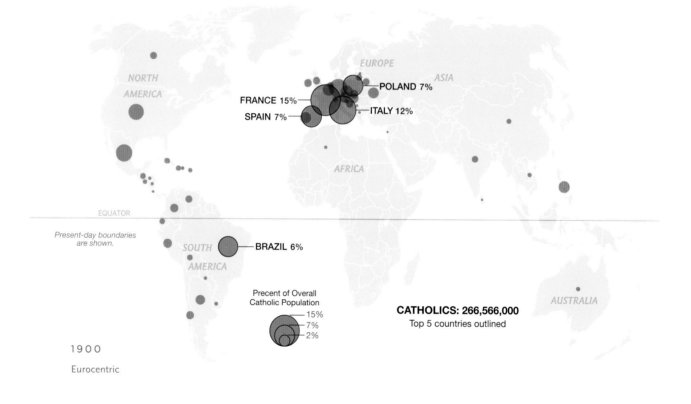

POLAND 7%

FRANCE 15%

ITALY 12%

SPAIN 7%

EQUATOR

Present-day boundaries are shown.

BRAZIL 6%

Precent of Overall Catholic Population

— 15%
— 7%
— 2%

CATHOLICS: 266,566,000
Top 5 countries outlined

1900

Eurocentric

SOURCES:

Maps: Numbers and statistics compiled from the World Christian Database.

Text: Pew Research Center. "The Global Catholic Population," February 2013.
Available online at www.pewforum.org/2013/02/13/the-global-catholic-population.

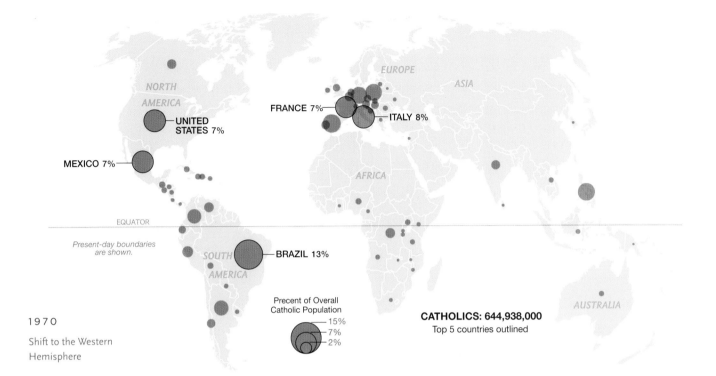

FRANCE 7%

UNITED
STATES 7%

MEXICO 7%

ITALY 8%

EQUATOR

*Present-day boundaries
are shown.*

BRAZIL 13%

Precent of Overall
Catholic Population

15%
7%
2%

CATHOLICS: 644,938,000
Top 5 countries outlined

1970

Shift to the Western
Hemisphere

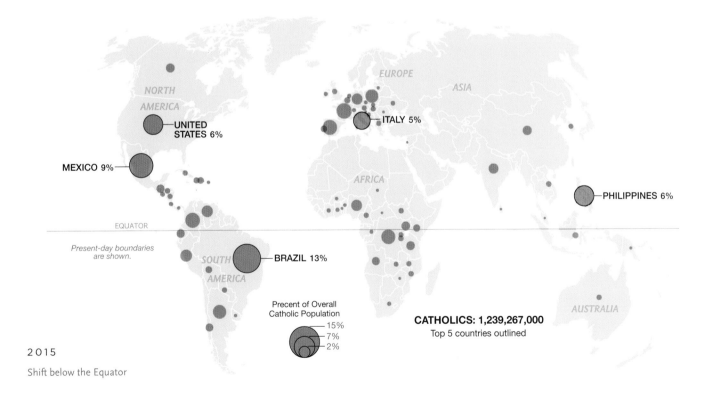

UNITED
STATES 6%

MEXICO 9%

ITALY 5%

PHILIPPINES 6%

EQUATOR

*Present-day boundaries
are shown.*

BRAZIL 13%

Precent of Overall
Catholic Population

15%
7%
2%

CATHOLICS: 1,239,267,000
Top 5 countries outlined

2015

Shift below the Equator

LIST OF POPES

St. Peter *(d. c. 64)*

St. Linus *(c. 66-c. 78)*

St. Anacletus *(c. 79-c. 91)*

St. Clement I *(c. 91-c. 101)*

St. Evaristus *(c. 100-c. 109)*

St. Alexander I *(c. 109-c. 116)*

St. Sixtus I *(c. 116-c. 125)*

St. Telesphorus *(c. 125-c. 136)*

St. Hyginus *(c. 138-c. 142)*

St. Pius I *(c. 142-c. 155)*

St. Anicetus *(c. 155-c. 166)*

St. Soter *(c. 166-c. 174)*

St. Eleutherius, or Eleutherus *(c. 174-89)*

St. Victor I *(189-98)*

St. Zephyrinus *(198/9-217)*

St. Callistus I *(often Calixtus) (217-22)*

St. Urban I *(222-30)*

St. Pontian *(21 July 230-28 Sept. 235)*

St. Anterus *(21 Nov. 235-3 Jan. 236)*

St. Fabian *(10 Jan. 236-20 Jan. 250)*

St. Cornelius *(Mar. 251-June 253)*

St. Lucius I *(25 June 253-5 Mar. 254)*

St. Stephen I *(12 May 254-2 Aug. 257)*

St. Sixtus II *(Aug. 257-6 Aug. 258)*

St. Dionysius *(22 July 260-26 Dec. 268)*

St. Felix I *(3 Jan. 269-30 Dec. 274)*

St. Eutychian *(4 Jan. 275-7 Dec. 283)*

St. Gaius, or Caius *(17 Dec. 283-22 Apr. 296)*

St. Marcellinus *(30 June 296-? 304; d. 25 Oct. 304)*

St. Marcellus I *(Nov./Dec. 306-16 Jan. 308)*

St. Eusebius *(18 Apr.-21 Oct. 310)*

St. Miltiades, or Melchiades *(2 July 311-10 Jan. 314)*

St. Silvester I *(31 Jan. 314-31 Dec. 335)*

St. Mark *(18 Jan.-7 Oct. 336)*

St. Julius I *(6 Feb. 337-12 Apr. 352)*

Liberius *(17 May 352-24 Sept. 366)*

St. Damasus I *(1 Oct. 366-11 Dec. 384)*

St. Siricius *(Dec. 384-26 Nov. 399)*

St. Anastasius I *(27 Nov. 399-19 Dec. 401)*

St. Innocent I *(21 Dec. 401-12 Mar. 417)*

St. Zosimus *(18 Mar. 417-26 Dec. 418)*

St. Boniface I *(28 Dec. 418-4 Sept. 422)*

St. Celestine I *(10 Sept. 422-27 July 432)*

St. Sixtus, or Xystus III *(31 July 432-19 Aug. 440)*

St. Leo I *(Aug./Sept. 440-10 Nov. 461)*

St. Hilarus *(19 Nov. 461-29 Feb. 468)*

St. Simplicius *(3 Mar. 468-10 Mar. 483)*

St. Felix III *(II) (13 Mar. 483-1 Mar. 492)*

St. Gelasius I *(1 Mar. 492-21 Nov. 496)*

Anastasius II *(24 Nov. 496-19 Nov. 498)*

St. Symmachus *(22 Nov. 498-19 July 514)*

St. Hormisdas *(20 July 514-6 Aug. 523)*

St. John I *(13 Aug. 523-18 May 526)*

St. Felix IV *(III) (12 July 526-22 Sept. 530)*

Boniface II *(22 Sept. 530-17 Oct. 532)*

John II *(2 Jan. 533-8 May 535)*

St. Agapitus I *(13 May 535-22 Apr. 536)*

St. Silverius *(8 June 536-11 Nov. 537; d. 2 Dec. 537)*

Vigilius *(29 Mar. 537-7 June 555)*

Pelagius I *(16 Apr. 556-3 Mar. 561)*

John III *(17 July 561-13 July 574)*

Benedict I *(2 June 575-30 July 579)*

Pelagius II *(26 Nov. 579-7 Feb. 590)*

St. Gregory I *(3 Sept. 590-12 Mar. 604)*

Sabinian *(13 Sept. 604-22 Feb. 606)*

Boniface III *(19 Feb.-12 Nov. 607)*

St. Boniface IV *(15 Sept. 608-8 May 615)*

St. Deusdedit *(later Adeodatus I) (19 Oct. 615-8 Nov. 618)*

Boniface V *(23 Dec. 619-25 Oct. 625)*

Honorius I *(27 Oct. 625-12 Oct. 638)*

Severinus *(28 May-2 Aug. 640)*

John IV *(24 Dec. 640-12 Oct. 642)*

Theodore I *(24 Nov. 642-14 May 649)*

St. Martin I *(5 July 649-17 June 653; d. 16 Sept. 655)*

St. Eugene I *(10 Aug. 654-2 June 657)*

St. Vitalian *(30 July 657-27 Jan. 672)*

Adeodatus II *(11 Apr. 672-17 June 676)*

Donus *(2 Nov. 676-11 Apr. 678)*

St. Agatho *(27 June 678-10 Jan. 681)*

St. Leo II *(17 Aug. 682-3 July 683)*

St. Benedict II *(26 June 684-8 May 685)*

John V *(23 July 685-2 Aug. 686)*

Conon *(21 Oct. 686-21 Sept. 687)*

St. Sergius I *(15 Dec. 687-9 Sept. 701)*

John VI *(30 Oct. 701-11 Jan. 705)*

John VII *(1 Mar. 705-18 Oct. 707)*

Sisinnius *(15 Jan.-4 Feb. 708)*

Constantine *(25 Mar. 708-9 Apr. 715)*

St. Gregory II *(19 May 715-11 Feb. 731)*

St. Gregory III *(18 Mar. 731-28 Nov. 741)*

St. Zacharias *(3 Dec. 741-15 Mar. 752)*

Stephen *(II) (22 or 23-25 or 26 Mar. 752)*

Stephen II *(III) (26 Mar. 752-26 Apr. 757)*

St. Paul I *(29 May 757-28 June 767)*

Stephen III *(IV) (7 Aug. 768-24 Jan. 772)*

Hadrian I *(1 Feb. 772-25 Dec. 795)*

St. Leo III *(26 Dec. 795-12 June 816)*

Stephen IV *(V) (22 June 816-24 Jan. 817)*

St. Paschal I *(24 Jan. 817-11 Feb. 824)*

Eugene II *(5? June 824-27? Aug. 827)*

Valentine *(Aug.-Sept. 827)*

Gregory IV *(late 827-25 Jan. 844)*

Sergius II *(Jan. 844-27 Jan. 847)*

St. Leo IV *(10 Apr. 847-17 July 855)*

Benedict III *(29 Sept. 855-17 Apr. 858)*

St. Nicholas I *(24 Apr. 858-13 Nov. 867)*

Hadrian II *(14 Dec. 867-Nov. or Dec. 872)*

John VIII *(14 Dec. 872-16 Dec. 882)*

Marinus I *(16 Dec. 882-15 May 884)*

St. Hadrian III *(17 May 884-mid-Sept. 885)*

Stephen V *(VI) (Sept. 885-14 Sept. 891)*

Formosus *(6 Oct. 891-4 Apr. 896)*

Boniface VI *(Apr. 896)*

Stephen VI *(VII) (May 896-Aug. 897)*

Romanus *(Aug.-Nov. 897; d. ?)*

Theodore II *(Nov. 897)*

John IX *(Jan. 898-Jan. 900)*

Benedict IV *(May/June 900-Aug. 903)*

Leo V *(Aug.-Sept. 903; d. early 904)*

Sergius III *(29 Jan. 904-14 Apr. 911)*

Anastasius III *(c. June 911-c. Aug. 913)*

Lando *(c. Aug. 913-c. Mar. 914)*

John X *(Mar./Apr. 914-deposed May 928; d. 929)*

Leo VI *(May-Dec. 928)*

Stephen VII *(VIII) (Dec. 928-Feb. 931)*

John XI *(Feb. or Mar. 931-Dec. 935 or Jan. 936)*

Leo VII *(3 Jan. 936-13 July 939)*

Stephen VIII *(IX) (14 July 939-late Oct. 942)*

Marinus II *(30 Oct. 942-early May 946)*

Agapitus II *(10 May 946-Dec. 955)*

John XII *(16 Dec. 955-14 May 964)*

Leo VIII *(4 Dec. 963-1 Mar. 965)*

Benedict V *(22 May-deposed 23 June 964; d. 4 July 966)*

John XIII *(1 Oct. 965-6 Sept. 972)*

Benedict VI *(19 Jan. 973-July 974)*

Benedict VII (Oct. 974-10 July 983)

John XIV (Dec. 983-20 Aug. 984)

John XV (mid-Aug. 985-Mar. 996)

Gregory V (3 May 996-18 Feb. 999)

Sylvester II (2 Apr. 999-12 May 1003)

John XVII (16 May-6 Nov. 1003)

John XVIII (25 Dec. 1003-June or July 1009)

Sergius IV (31 July 1009-12 May 1012)

Benedict VIII (17 May 1012-9 Apr. 1024)

John XIX (19 Apr. 1024-20 Oct. 1032)

Benedict IX (21 Oct. 1032-Sept. 1044; 10 Mar.-1 May 1045; 8 Nov. 1047-16 July 1048; d. 1055/6)

Silvester III (20 Jan.-10 Mar. 1045; d. 1063)

Gregory VI (1 May 1045-20 Dec. 1046; d. late 1047)

Clement II (24 Dec. 1046-9 Oct. 1047)

Damasus II (17 July-9 Aug. 1048)

St. Leo IX (12 Feb. 1049-19 Apr. 1054)

Victor II (13 Apr. 1055-28 July 1057)

Stephen IX (X) (2 Aug. 1057-29 Mar. 1058)

Nicholas II (6 Dec. 1058-19 or 26 July 1061)

Alexander II (30 Sept. 1061-21 Apr. 1073)

St. Gregory VII (22 Apr. 1073-25 May 1085)

Bl. Victor III (24 May 1086; 9 May-16 Sept. 1087)

Bl. Urban II (12 Mar. 1088-29 July 1099)

Paschal II (13 Aug. 1099-21 Jan. 1118)

Gelasius II (24 Jan. 1118-29 Jan. 1119)

Callistus II (2 Feb. 1119-14 Dec. 1124)

Celestine (II) (15/16 Dec. 1124; d. 1125/6)

Honorius II (21 Dec. 1124-13 Feb. 1130)

Innocent II (14 Feb. 1130-24 Sept. 1143)

Celestine II (26 Sept. 1143-8 Mar. 1144)

Lucius II (12 Mar. 1144-15 Feb. 1145)

Bl. Eugene III (15 Feb. 1145-8 July 1153)

Anastasius IV (8 July 1153-3 Dec. 1154)

Hadrian IV (4 Dec. 1154-1 Sept. 1159)

Alexander III (7 Sept. 1159-30 Aug. 1181)

Lucius III (1 Sept. 1181-25 Nov. 1185)

Urban III (25 Nov. 1185-19/20 Oct. 1187)

Gregory VIII (21 Oct.-17 Dec. 1187)

Clement III (19 Dec. 1187-late Mar. 1191)

Celestine III (Mar./Apr. 1191-8 Jan. 1198)

Innocent III (8 Jan. 1198-16 July 1216)

Honorius III (18 July 1216-18 Mar. 1227)

Gregory IX (19 Mar. 1227-22 Aug. 1241)

Celestine IV (25 Oct.-10 Nov. 1241)

Innocent IV (25 June 1243-7 Dec. 1254)

Alexander IV (12 Dec. 1254-25 May 1261)

Urban IV (29 Aug. 1261-2 Oct. 1264)

Clement IV (5 Feb. 1265-29 Nov. 1268)

Bl. Gregory X (1 Sept. 1271-10 Jan. 1276)

Bl. Innocent V (21 Jan.-22 June 1276)

Hadrian V (11 July-18 Aug. 1276)

John XXI (8 Sept. 1276-20 May 1277)

Nicholas III (25 Nov. 1277-22 Aug. 1280)

Martin IV (22 Feb. 1281-28 Mar. 1285)

Honorius IV (2 Apr. 1285-3 Apr. 1287)

Nicholas IV (22 Feb. 1288-4 Apr. 1292)

St. Peter Celestine V (5 July-13 Dec. 1294; d. 19 May 1296)

Boniface VIII (24 Dec. 1294-11 Oct. 1303)

Bl. Benedict XI (22 Oct. 1303-7 July 1304)

Clement V (5 June 1305-20 Apr. 1314)

John XXII (7 Aug. 1316-4 Dec. 1334)

Benedict XII (20 Dec. 1334-25 Apr. 1342)

Clement VI (7 May 1342-6 Dec. 1352)

Innocent VI (18 Dec. 1352-12 Sept. 1362)

Bl. Urban V (28 Sept. 1362-19 Dec. 1370)

Gregory XI (30 Dec. 1370-27 Mar. 1378)

Urban VI (8 Apr. 1378-15 Oct. 1389)

Boniface IX (2 Nov. 1389-1 Oct. 1404)

Innocent VII (17 Oct. 1404-6 Nov. 1406)

Gregory XII (30 Nov. 1406-4 July 1415; d. 18 Oct. 1417)

Martin V (11 Nov. 1417-20 Feb. 1431)

Eugene IV (3 Mar. 1431-23 Feb. 1447)

Nicholas V (6 Mar. 1447-24 Mar. 1455)

Callistus III (8 Apr. 1455-6 Aug. 1458)

Pius II (19 Aug. 1458-15 Aug. 1464)

Paul II (30 Aug. 1464-26 July 1471)

Sixtus IV (9 Aug. 1471-12 Aug. 1484)

Innocent VIII (29 Aug. 1484-25 July 1492)

Alexander VI (11 Aug. 1492-18 Aug. 1503)

Pius III (22 Sept.-18 Oct. 1503)

Julius II (1 Nov. 1503-21 Feb. 1513)

Leo X (11 Mar. 1513-1 Dec. 1521)

Hadrian VI (9 Jan. 1522-14 Sept. 1523)

Clement VII (19 Nov. 1523-25 Sept. 1534)

Paul III (13 Oct. 1534-10 Nov. 1549)

Julius III (8 Feb. 1550-23 Mar. 1555)

Marcellus II (9 Apr.-1 May 1555)

Paul IV (23 May 1555-18 Aug. 1559)

Pius IV (25 Dec. 1559-9 Dec. 1565)

St. Pius V (7 Jan. 1566-1 May 1572)

Gregory XIII (14 May 1572-10 Apr. 1585)

Sixtus V (24 Apr. 1585-27 Aug. 1590)

Urban VII (15-27 Sept. 1590)

Gregory XIV (5 Dec. 1590-16 Oct. 1591)

Innocent IX (29 Oct.-30 Dec. 1591)

Clement VIII (30 Jan. 1592-5 Mar. 1605)

Leo XI (1-27 Apr. 1605)

Paul V (16 May 1605-28 Jan. 1621)

Gregory XV (9 Feb. 1621-8 July 1623)

Urban VIII (6 Aug. 1623-29 July 1644)

Innocent X (15 Sept. 1644-1 Jan. 1655)

Alexander VII (7 Apr. 1655-22 May 1667)

Clement IX (20 June 1667-9 Dec. 1669)

Clement X (29 Apr. 1670-22 July 1676)

Bl. Innocent XI (21 Sept. 1676-12 Aug. 1689)

Alexander VIII (6 Oct. 1689-1 Feb. 1691)

Innocent XII (12 July 1691-27 Sept. 1700)

Clement XI (23 Nov. 1700-19 Mar. 1721)

Innocent XIII (8 May 1721-7 Mar. 1724)

Benedict XIII (29 May 1724-21 Feb. 1730)

Clement XII (12 July 1730-6 Feb. 1740)

Benedict XIV (17 Aug. 1740-3 May 1758)

Clement XIII (6 July 1758-2 Feb. 1769)

Clement XIV (19 May 1769-22 Sept. 1774)

Pius VI (15 Feb. 1775-29 Aug. 1799)

Pius VII (14 Mar. 1800-20 July 1823)

Leo XII (28 Sept. 1823-10 Feb. 1829)

Pius VIII (31 Mar. 1829-30 Nov. 1830)

Gregory XVI (2 Feb. 1831-1 June 1846)

Bl. Pius IX (16 June 1846-7 Feb. 1878)

Leo XIII (20 Feb. 1878-20 July 1903)

St. Pius X (4 Aug. 1903-20 Aug. 1914)

Benedict XV (3 Sept. 1914-22 Jan. 1922)

Pius XI (6 Feb. 1922-10 Feb. 1939)

Pius XII (2 Mar. 1939-9 Oct. 1958)

St. John XXIII (28 Oct. 1958-3 June 1963)

Paul VI (21 June 1963-6 Aug. 1978)

John Paul I (26 Aug.-28 Sept. 1978)

St. John Paul II (16 Oct. 1978-2 Apr. 2005)

Benedict XVI (19 Apr. 2005-28 Feb. 2013)

Francis (13 Mar. 2013-)

ACKNOWLEDGMENTS

DAVE YODER

This book was made possible with the help of numerous supporters who put me in the position to take these photographs.

I first thank Pope Francis for his patience in accepting another photographer in his crowded vicinity.

Additional thanks go to:

Ambassador Kenneth F. Hackett and his wife, Joan, as well as Ambassador David Lane, who enthusiastically supported National Geographic's efforts.

The remarkable photographers of *l'Osservatore Romano*, who took me under their wing. I am proud to call them friends. This book would not exist without the help of Francesco Sforza, Simone Risoluti, and Mario Tomassetti, who showed me how to be a better photographer. Permission for their assistance was generously given by Don Sergio Pellini, director of *l'Osservatore Romano*.

Archbishop Claudio Maria Celli, Monsignor Paul Tighe, Laura Riccioni, and Francesco Macrì, of the Pontifical Council for Social Communications, who dutifully shepherded me through the course of the assignment.

The countless people working within the borders of Vatican City who trusted me and allowed me to work freely.

National Geographic Chief Content Officer Chris Johns, Editor in Chief Susan Goldberg, and Director of Photography Sarah Leen for entrusting me with the project, and Elizabeth Krist for her inexhaustible effort and guidance as my editor.

Linda Douglass and Ambassador John Phillips, for their support and friendship, which preceded this assignment by many years. They are family to me and greatly aided in the opportunity to create this book.

And to my father, who missed seeing this book by a few months.

ROBERT DRAPER

I'd like to express my deep indebtedness to the dozens of friends, associates, and close observers of Pope Francis in Rome, Argentina, and the United States whose insights and recollections proved crucial to this book. Additional thanks are due Ambassadors Kenneth F. Hackett, David Lane, and especially John Phillips and his wife, Linda Douglass, for their support and hospitality throughout my stays in Rome.

I thank as well my interpreter in Argentina, Tomas Hughes. Finally, I would like to thank *National Geographic* magazine Editor in Chief Susan Goldberg, my editor John Hoeffel, research editor Taryn Salinas, and National Geographic Books editors Anne Smyth and Barbara Payne for all of the support they lent to this project.

ABOUT THE PHOTOGRAPHER

Dave Yoder is a contributing photographer to *National Geographic* magazine and numerous other publications. His work has ranged widely in interests, from bounty hunters to a children's circus to a lost city in unexplored Honduras jungle—and to photographing Pope Francis. He was born in Goshen, Indiana, and lives in Italy.

ABOUT THE AUTHOR

Robert Draper is a contributing writer to *National Geographic* and the *New York Times Magazine*. His dozens of stories for *National Geographic*—which have taken him from Somalia to Sri Lanka to the Congo River—include the 2014 National Magazine Award–winning "Last Days of a Storm Chaser." He is the author of several books, including the *New York Times* bestseller *Dead Certain: The Presidency of George W. Bush*. Draper lives in Washington, D.C.

POPE FRANCIS AND THE NEW VATICAN

Dave Yoder
Robert Draper

PUBLISHED BY THE NATIONAL GEOGRAPHIC SOCIETY

Gary E. Knell, *President and Chief Executive Officer*
John M. Fahey, *Chairman of the Board*
Declan Moore, *Chief Media Officer*
Chris Johns, *Chief Content Officer*

PREPARED BY THE BOOK DIVISION

Hector Sierra, *Senior Vice President and General Manager*
Lisa Thomas, *Senior Vice President and Editorial Director*
Jonathan Halling, *Creative Director*
Marianne R. Koszorus, *Design Director*
R. Gary Colbert, *Production Director*
Jennifer A. Thornton, *Director of Managing Editorial*
Susan S. Blair, *Director of Photography*
Meredith C. Wilcox, *Director, Administration and Rights Clearance*

STAFF FOR THIS BOOK

Anne Smyth, *Project Editor*
Barbara Payne, *Consulting Editor*
Elizabeth Krist, *Illustrations Editor*
Charles Kogod, *Illustrations Editor*
Moira Haney, *Illustrations Editor*
Marty Ittner, *Art Director*
Carl Mehler, *Director of Maps*
Gus Platis, *Map Editor*
Lauren E. James, *Map Research and Production*
Jason Treat, *Senior Graphics Editor*
Kelsey Nowakowski, *Graphics and Arts Researcher*
Maia Wachtel, *Graphics Research Intern*
Patrick Bagley, *Assistant Illustrations Editor*
Michelle R. Harris, *Legends Writer*
Zachary Galasi, *Researcher*
Marshall Kiker, *Associate Managing Editor*
Judith Klein, *Senior Production Editor*
Mike Horenstein, *Production Manager*
Katie Olsen, *Design Production Specialist*
Nicole Miller, *Design Production Assistant*
Darrick McRae, *Manager, Production Services*
Michael G. Lappin, *Imaging*
Agnès Tabah, *Legal Counsel*

ILLUSTRATIONS CREDITS

All photos by Dave Yoder unless otherwise noted below.

78-79, AP Photo/Pablo Leguizamon, File; 83, Filippo Fiorini/Demotix/Corbis; 84, Filippo Fiorini/Demotix/Corbis; 87, Grupo44/STR/Getty Images; 88-89, GDA via AP Images; 91, AP Photo/El Salvador School; 92, REUTERS/Parroquia Virgen de Caacupe/Handout; 94-95, AP Photo/DyN; 96, Claudia Conteris/AFP/Getty Images; 99, REUTERS/Enrique Marcarian; 100, Lalo Yasky/Getty Images; 152, Victor Boswell/National Geographic Creative; 190-191, AP Photo/Jorge Saenz; 192, Marcelo Tasso/AFP/Getty Images; 198, Doug Mills/The New York Times/Redux Pictures; 201, AP Photo/Oded Balilty; 202-203, REUTERS/Ricardo Moraes; 210, Ozan Kose/AFP/Getty Images.

Pages 246–247:

Text sources: Eamon Duffy, *Saints and Sinners: A History of the Popes*. Yale University Press, 1997. James Weiss, Associate Professor of Church History, Boston College Theology Department.

Image credits: (by row, from top): Museo Nacional Del Prado/Art Resource, NY; Album/Art Resource, NY (two images); Rmn-Grand Palais/Art Resource, NY; Gianni Dagli Orti, Art Archive at Art Resource, NY; Alfredo Dagli Orti, Art Archive at Art Resource, NY; Culture Club/Getty Images.

The National Geographic Society is one of the world's largest nonprofit scientific and educational organizations. Founded in 1888 to "increase and diffuse geographic knowledge," the member-supported Society works to inspire people to care about the planet. Through its online community, members can get closer to explorers and photographers, connect with other members around the world, and help make a difference. National Geographic reflects the world through its magazines, television programs, films, music and radio, books, DVDs, maps, exhibitions, live events, school publishing programs, interactive media, and merchandise. *National Geographic* magazine, the Society's official journal, published in English and 38 local-language editions, is read by more than 60 million people each month. The National Geographic Channel reaches 440 million households in 171 countries in 38 languages. National Geographic Digital Media receives more than 25 million visitors a month. National Geographic has funded more than 10,000 scientific research, conservation, and exploration projects and supports an education program promoting geography literacy. For more information, visit www.nationalgeographic.com.

For more information, please call 1-800-NGS LINE (647-5463) or write to the following address:

National Geographic Society
1145 17th Street NW
Washington, D.C. 20036-4688 U.S.A.

Your purchase supports our nonprofit work and makes you part of our global community. Thank you for sharing our belief in the power of science, exploration and storytelling to change the world. To activate your member benefits, complete your free membership profile at natgeo.com/joinnow.

For information about special discounts for bulk purchases, please contact National Geographic Books Special Sales: ngspecsales@ngs.org

For rights or permissions inquiries, please contact National Geographic Books Subsidiary Rights: ngbookrights@ngs.org

LIBRARY OF CONGRESS CATALOGING-IN-PUBLICATION DATA

Draper, Robert.
  Pope Francis and the new Vatican / essays by Robert Draper ; photos by Dave Yoder. -- 1st [edition].
    pages cm
  ISBN 978-1-4262-1582-7 (hardcover : alk. paper) --
ISBN 978-1-4262-1583-4 (hardcover (deluxe edition) : alk. paper)
  1. Francis, Pope, 1936- I. Title.

  BX1378.7.D73 2015
  282.092--dc23

                    2015013122

Printed in the United States of America
15/QGT-CML/1